THE DEMISE OF NIGERIA AIRWAYS LIMITED

DISCLAIMER

The purpose of writing this book is to preserve the name and image of the defunct national airline, Nigeria Airways, and to remind readers that the nation once had a national airline with the emblem of an elephant, which should be remembered and passed on to future generations.

When writing about an institution of such national prestige without representing its management or the Federal Ministry of Aviation and Aerospace, my insights may be limited. It is possible that some individuals may view the events and situations described from a different perspective.

I want to clarify that my intention is not to insult, humiliate, or ridicule anyone. I apologise to anyone who may feel offended, as this was not my objective. My aim is simply to shed light on some internal issues within the airline that were not widely known to the public.

Finally, I urge the government to recognise the plight of the former employees of Nigeria Airways, who continue to suffer. If the pensions approved by the previous administration of President Buhari were paid, it would greatly alleviate their situation. I hope this will prompt President Tinubu to take action and facilitate discussions on how these workers can be included in the regular monthly pension scheme.

God bless Nigeria.

THE DEMISE OF NIGERIA AIRWAYS LIMITED

OLATUNJI OLUSANYA

BABA JOOOO

THE DEMISE OF NIGERIA AIRWAYS LIMITED
By Olatunji Olusanya

Copyright © 2024 by Olatunji Olusanya

Published by Baruch Publishing - 07908684207
Contact Copyright Holder at
Olatunji Olusanya
Email: tunjato45@yahoo.com
Tel: 07403 232433

All rights are reserved. No part of this publication may be reproduced, stored in a retrieval system or transmitted in any form or by any means, electronic, mechanical, photocopying, recording or otherwise, without prior permission of Olatunji Olusanya

Cover & Interior Design by Karl Hunt

ISBN 979-8-89587-697-8

CONTENTS

Dedication   ix
Preface   xi
Introduction   xiii

CHAPTER ONE: Origin of Nigeria Airways Limited   1

CHAPTER TWO: What Made Nigeria Airways Ltd Different from Other Federal or State Parastatals or Corporations   9

CHAPTER THREE: The Objectives and Government Uses of Nigeria Airways   15

CHAPTER FOUR: The Supervisory of the Federal Ministry of Aviation Over Nigeria Airways   23

CHAPTER FIVE: External Powers that Formulate Policies on Nigeria Airways   37

CHAPTER SIX: External Influences within Nigeria   46

CHAPTER SEVEN: To Become an Aviation Pilot   54

CHAPTER EIGHT: Managing Nigeria Airways Ltd   64

CHAPTER NINE: Board of Directors — 70

CHAPTER TEN: How MD/Directors Were Appointed and Removed — 75

CHAPTER ELEVEN: The Roles of Air Ticket Agents — 87

CHAPTER TWELVE: Contracts Award — 95

CHAPTER THIRTEEN: Staff Concessional Travel Tickets — 100

CHAPTER FOURTEEN: V.I.P Concessional Tickets — 114

CHAPTER FIFTEEN: Purchase of Aircraft for the Airline — 127

CHAPTER SIXTEEN: Workers Unions Contributions — 135

CHAPTER SEVENTEEN: Catering Services — 144

CHAPTER EIGHTEEN: The Dutch Airline (KLM) — 149

CHAPTER NINETEEN: Sales of Boeing F. 28 Aircraft — 155

CHAPTER TWENTY: The Annual Hajj Operations — 158

CHAPTER TWENTY-ONE: Abandoned Aircraft at Air Lingus Hanger in Ireland — 167

CHAPTER TWENTY-TWO: December Retrenchment Trauma — 178

CHAPTER TWENTY-THREE: Inhumanity at Workplace — 192

CHAPTER TWENTY-FOUR: Nigeria Airways Accident Records — 202

CHAPTER TWENTY-FIVE: The Virtues of National Integrity — 211

CONTENTS

CHAPTER TWENTY-SIX: Staff Social Activities at Sports Club   218

CHAPTER TWENTY-SEVEN: Issues of Certificate Verifications and Ghost Workers   225

CHAPTER TWENTY-EIGHT: Who Owns the Gra Ikeja?   229

CHAPTER TWENTY-NINE: Federal Ministry of Aviation—A Milking Cow   239

CHAPTER THIRTY: Life of Pensioners of Nigeria Airways   251

CHAPTER THIRTY-ONE: My Transverse Journeys in Nigeria Airways   267

About the Author   280

DEDICATION

I WOULD BE ungrateful if I failed to dedicate this book to a man who embodied fairness, integrity, and courage, one who confronted challenges head-on. Sadly, he is no longer with us to witness the fruits of his hard work in Nigeria Airways. This book is dedicated to Mr Tunji Otunuyi, who served as a Principal Assistant to Alhaji Bature during his tenure as Director of Personnel. Mr Otunuyi chaired the panel that interviewed me when I applied for employment with the airline. Despite receiving direct instructions from Mr Adegoke, one of the department's controllers, regarding selecting specific candidates, Otunuyi stood his ground. He refused to compromise the panel's recommendations and welcomed my acceptance of a Grade Level 07 offer, even though the budget could have allowed for Grade Level 09.

Tragically, Mr Otunuyi was shot dead inside his car at a junction in Epe while returning to Lagos on a Sunday afternoon after visiting his family. May the Lord grant his gentle and righteous soul eternal rest in His bosom, and may He give his family the strength to bear this irreplaceable loss. His passing remains a deep and painful memory.

I also dedicate this book to Mr Sunday Epoyun, a secretary in the Chairman's office, whose assistance ensured my name was added to the list of candidates invited for the interview. May the Lord bless you abundantly in all your endeavours, just as you were a blessing to me.

Most importantly, this book is dedicated to the former workers of Nigeria Airways, who were forcefully retired without proper plans for their gratuities or pensions. Many of you have tragically lost your lives to curable illnesses, because, in Nigeria, without money, one cannot see a doctor or afford necessary medications.

May the Lord move Mr Keyamo, our current Minister of Aviation and Aerospace, to release the remaining ₦36 billion approved by former President Muhammadu Buhari (Rtd) for payment to the retired employees. For those suffering from multiple illnesses, I pray that the God who healed the woman with the issue of blood after 12 years will touch and heal you all.

Lastly, if the workers of NAA, NAHCO, and FCAA, sister companies under the Federal Ministry of Aviation, are granted monthly pensions, the same right must be extended to the former workers of Nigeria Airways.

We are all Nigerians, and we all share the same DIGESTIVE SYSTEM.

PREFACE

THE ART OF writing a book is not about pleasing the writer, proving superiority, or showcasing greater knowledge. Writing with such intentions only feeds an ego that thrives in the illusion of power. This book, instead, serves as a form of self-explanation. It aims to provide clarity for those within the organisation and the public at large about matters within other departments, problems that the Public Relations Section of the airline never dared to reveal.

Our goal is to offer readers and buyers a book they will feel was worth the price they paid. When reading something of historical significance, one might even forget about everyday routines, such as missing lunch, because each page presents unexpected insights.

It is human nature to form opinions based on the author's name, especially when that name is as renowned as Tai Solarin with "Mayflower", Wole Soyinka with "The Man Died", or Chinua Achebe with "Things Fall Apart". Like these works, this book attempts to make its mark by addressing significant historical matters.

Some airline staff may have more expertise in specific areas than I do, and they were encouraged to share their perspectives to enrich the collective understanding of the airline's operations. What I present here is rooted in fact, and supported by evidence beyond reasonable doubt. As we all know, truth can be bitter, and some may find parts of this book uncomfortable. Yet, it is better to speak the truth and shame the devil than to remain silent.

Writing about an essential government institution like Nigeria Airways was not an easy undertaking. It required careful attention to accuracy, ensuring that no individual or position was unfairly portrayed as criminal or insignificant. Balancing this narrative without stepping on a few toes was a challenge, hence my disclaimer at the start of the book.

I am grateful to my publisher and the editorial team, whose efforts reduced the book's size from nearly 400 pages to its present form. As they understood, it is not the volume but the quality and conciseness that matter to readers.

When a book addresses national issues, it may earn both admiration and criticism. If readers appreciate the work, they may express their gratitude, even through letters from strangers. But in our African context, it is equally likely that some will criticise, call you names, and attempt to diminish your efforts.

Whatever responses this book receives will be part of my growth as a writer. Every bit of feedback, positive or negative, will only sharpen my ability to do better in the future.

INTRODUCTION

THIS BOOK ADDRESSES national issues that affect every citizen of our country, directly or indirectly. No matter who you are or which state in the Federation you come from, you must have heard of Nigeria Airways Limited.

The economic challenges we face today are undeniable. Many of us have relatives who have "Japa"—leaving Nigeria in search of greener pastures abroad. Despite having over 15,000 universities across the nation, each potentially graduating 1,000 students annually, the employment market grows by 150,000 new graduates every year. However, with insufficient employment opportunities and essential infrastructure, many companies that could have absorbed these graduates have either folded up or relocated abroad.

Consider the case of the Volkswagen factory in Lagos and the Peugeot plant in Kaduna, both have shut down operations. The textile industry, once a massive employer of millions, has moved to countries like Ghana and South Africa. More troubling is how China now manufactures Kampala fabrics and exports them to Nigeria. I even heard that China is exporting melon-cooked soup to us. Similarly, Malaysia took cassava and palm seedlings from Nigeria in the 1990s, and today they export gari and palm oil to African nations, including Nigeria.

These harsh realities are why many master's degree holders are forced to become motorcycle riders to earn a living. The Federal Government is also reported to owe millions of dollars to foreign airlines, leading many of them to suspend operations in Nigeria. Only recently did Emirates Airlines resume services to the country after pulling out in protest.

The focus of this book is to illuminate how the Federal Government, despite founding and owning Nigeria Airways, allowed mismanagement to destroy the airline. Appointed officials, tasked with managing the airline, made poor decisions that favoured private airlines, dooming Nigeria Airways to failure. For example, the Federal Civil Aviation Authority (FCAA) deliberately scheduled early flights for private airlines while grounding Nigeria Airways until the afternoon, cutting it off from lucrative routes like Abuja, Kaduna, Kano, and Port Harcourt. This was a slow, calculated death for the national airline.

The final blow came when President Olusegun Obasanjo and his Vice President, Atiku Abubakar, unceremoniously shut down the airline. Without transparency, they liquidated Nigeria Airways, even ordering Mobile Police (MOPOL) to seize and burn vital documents tracing aircraft purchases dating back to 1958. Eventually, Nigeria Airways (House) was handed over to Arik Air, but without clear agreements on payments or contracts with the government. The fate of the liquidated pension fund remains shrouded in secrecy.

INTRODUCTION

No concrete plans were made to compensate staff for their pensions. Even the partial pension approved by President Muhammadu Buhari in 2018 was only 50% paid, and the remaining funds reportedly ₦36 billion, are still outstanding. Some fear that these unpaid funds may have been laundered, as alleged in a scandal involving the Accountant General of the Federation.

Meanwhile, many former airline staff members have died from treatable illnesses because they could not afford medical care. Desperation has led surviving employees to gather regularly for joint Christian and Muslim prayers near the old catering site by the Nigerian Air Force base. Though the current Minister of Aviation and Aerospace is aware of their plight, efforts to secure the outstanding payments have been insufficient.

This book is a call to action, a reminder that we are all Nigerians, bound by the Constitution and that the suffering of our fellow citizens demands accountability and justice.

Potsluchy

CHAPTER ONE

ORIGIN OF NIGERIA AIRWAYS LIMITED

I COULD REMEMBER when most companies in Nigeria, either directly owned or financed by the government, were referred to as parastatals or corporations. These entities, often supervised by ministries, differed fundamentally from private companies. Unlike private firms, which bear limited liabilities in their names, these government-backed institutions did not, for they largely depended on government stakeholders for financing and oversight. Among these organisations, notable examples include the Nigerian National Petroleum Corporation (NNPC), which has since evolved into the Nigerian National Petroleum Corporation Limited (NNPCL) because of recent changes. Other examples include the Central Bank of Nigeria (CBN), the National Insurance Corporation of Nigeria (NICN), the Nigeria Railway Corporation (NRC), the Nigerian Ports Authority (NPA), and the Nigerian Shipping Corporation (NSC), to name a few.

These government-owned corporations held distinct advantages. Their capital and infrastructure were invested by the state, and they were not expected to feel the burden of deficits. Should there be losses in their annual transactions, the government—whether at the federal or state level—would step in, by either covering the shortfall or allowing the corporations to use accumulated profits for expansion or diversification.

Historically, employment within these establishments was considered secure, regardless of the economic climate. This stability lasted until the military regime of General Murtala Muhammed, who introduced the first general retrenchment in 1976, forever altering the landscape of government employment.

But the heart of this reflection lies with the origin of Nigeria Airways Limited. When colonial Britain extended its rule over parts of Africa, particularly in West Africa, their indirect rule allowed them to govern while maintaining the appearance of traditional authority through local rulers. West African nations like The Gambia, Sierra Leone, the Gold Coast (now Ghana), and Nigeria were united under this system.

In addition to political control, the British recognised the need for a common transportation system that would link the colonies to each other and Britain itself. Thus, the West African Air Corporation (WAAC) was established in the 1940s, providing a means for the colonies to stay connected. National airports and aerodromes were built where planes could land, delivering passengers and goods alike.

As time passed, WAAC expanded, and its operations were commercialised. British Airways was entrusted with running passenger flights between Britain and these West African nations, eventually operating routes within the region itself. This marked the beginning of a new era in air travel, one that would soon give rise to Nigeria Airways Limited, an embodiment of the country's aviation aspirations and its place within the broader framework of the British Empire's colonial reach.

As political consciousness deepened among Africans, it became clear that the days of colonial rule were numbered, and the path to independence for these territories was inevitable. We were witnessing a transformation, not only in governance but in the economy as well. In addition to air travel, there was a thriving trade relationship between the colonial powers and their dependent territories. One of the earliest companies facilitating this commercial exchange in Nigeria was the United African Company (UAC), which handled a wide range of goods—from essential items to luxury products like textiles, building materials, and even educational resources.

The tide of independence started with the Gold Coast, now Ghana, which became the first African nation to break free in 1957. This historic moment ignited a wave of demands across West Africa, including calls for the dismantling of colonial air transport monopolies like the West African Airways Corporation (WAAC). It was vital for each newly independent state to control its air travel. Ghana became the first to establish its airline in July 4th 1958, and soon after, Nigeria followed suit in August 23rd 1958.

In Nigeria, the creation of Nigeria Airways Limited was a point of pride and a symbol of self-reliance. The goal was to ensure the airline operated independently of government funds, capable of sustaining itself while serving the national interest. However, as a national carrier, Nigeria Airways could not refuse government orders, especially in times of national crisis. The airline became part of the larger Federal Ministry of Aviation, and its operations were governed by national priorities.

From 1915 to 2023, the Federal Ministry of Aviation experienced changes, eventually merging with the Federal Ministry of Transport to form a combined Ministry of Transport and Aviation. The Federal Civil Aviation Authority (FCAA) was established to oversee and manage Nigeria's airspace, ensuring all fees collected from air traffic over Nigeria were properly managed.

Nigeria Airways was tasked with procuring and maintaining commercial aircraft for both passenger and cargo flights, serving both domestic and international routes wherever bilateral agreements existed. It was clear from these responsibilities that the airline's primary goal was to be profitable while also fulfilling any national obligations assigned by the government.

To achieve this balance, all airlines registered in Nigeria were placed under the supervision of the FCAA, which operated under the Ministry of Aviation. Although this authority was registered with the International Air Transport Association (IATA) based in Switzerland, its duties became increasingly complex as the aviation industry evolved globally.

Foreign airlines began to enter Nigeria, supporting foreign businesses by transporting personnel and goods. This was especially evident in the oil industry, where the movement of oil rig equipment in states like Delta, Bayelsa, and Rivers required specialised air transport. One of the most notable foreign airlines was Aero Contractors, known for its chartered flights, particularly for businesses operating in Nigeria's growing petroleum sector.

The Nigerian government's decision to open the skies to commercial airlines allowed Nigerian companies to join the industry. Initially, these airlines operated domestically but soon expanded to international routes, with licenses to carry passengers to Europe. Early players in this market included Kabo Airlines and Okada Airlines, while Aero Contractors transitioned from charter services to passenger flights.

This evolution in Nigeria's aviation sector reflected the broader changes sweeping through the country as it embraced independence and self-determination, determined to control its skies and future.

It was a time when air travel in Nigeria was growing, and the need for organised coordination became apparent. To prevent mid-air collisions and confusion on the runways during landing or take-offs, a governing body was essential to regulate this intricate dance of aeroplanes. The solution came in the form of a structured timetable—carefully displayed to indicate when each aircraft should leave the ground and when it would arrive at any airport across the country. This was not just a local requirement but aligned with the global regulations of the International Air Transport Association (IATA), which set the standards for safe flying.

The Federal Civil Aviation Authority (FCAA) held the monumental responsibility of scheduling flight movements. They alone determined when an aircraft could take off, the direction it should follow in the skies, and the exact moment another plane could land. However, once an aircraft was on the ground, the Nigerian Airport Authority (NAA) took over. It was their job to manage where planes should park and ensure that the airports ran smoothly.

The FCAA's handling of these duties—whether efficiently or not—would later become a topic of discussion, but one cannot ignore the fact that human biases played a role. It was common knowledge that certain airlines received more favourable schedules for early morning flights to lucrative destinations like Abuja, Kano, Kaduna, and Port Harcourt. These routes were prized, and securing them was no small feat, often influenced by the nuances of Nigerian politics and business.

The Nigerian Airport Authority was another critical player in this aviation sector. They were, in effect, the landlords of all the airports in Nigeria, maintaining and operating these critical infrastructures. I remember vividly when the Murtala Muhammed International Airport first opened its doors in 1977. It was a marvel of efficiency. I arrived there in May 1979, and the airport was so pristine, so well-run, that I could hardly believe I was still in Nigeria. The air conditioning created a cool, refreshing atmosphere, reminiscent of spring in Europe. For the first time in my travels across Africa, I felt a deep sense of pride in my homeland.

The airport itself was a sight to behold—beautiful both inside and out. The roads leading to it were smooth and well-maintained, and a toll gate stood guard, preventing unauthorised vehicles from using the airport as a shortcut to nearby markets. But that was then. What has happened to the airport in recent years is beyond disappointing. Scandals have plagued the Ministry of Aviation, with accusations of inflated contracts for airport improvements. Yet, despite the best efforts of the Economic and Financial Crimes Commission (EFCC), no one has been brought to justice. Instead, the culprits hop from one political party to another, evading accountability.

One particularly unsettling incident involved the airport's massive air conditioning units. These units, manufactured in Italy, were sent back for repairs, similar to the comprehensive "D" checks done on aircraft. But they never returned. Those who dared to ask questions did not live long enough to tell the tale. It was a story best left untouched—some things are safer left undisturbed.

The Federal Government's influence on Nigeria Airways was palpable through the Ministry of Aviation:

- They appointed and removed the airline's managing directors, often announcing such decisions on the 4 PM news.
- At times, the government would step in to pay off the airline's debts, especially when Nigeria's credibility on the international stage was at stake.
- The Board of Directors was often filled with political rejects, individuals who had lost favour during elections, only to be rewarded with cushy positions in the airline.
- The airline's Executive Directors, who headed various departments, were often promoted from within, but loyalty to the managing director was the most crucial qualification. Even the appointment of these directors required approval from the Federal Ministry of Aviation and sometimes the Head of Civil Service.

I recall how Brigadier Bajowa, a former army officer, wielded his influence to secure the appointment of Mr. Olaseinde Ogunkayode as Director of Human Resources, following a mass retrenchment in 1986. Bajowa's connections ran deep, allowing him to push through appointments that others could only dream of.

Nigeria Airways was, in many ways, a reflection of the country itself. Nepotism, tribalism, and favouritism were rampant, and promotions were often given based on whom you knew rather than what you knew. Transferring someone with no experience in human resources from corporate planning to become the director of that very department was not unusual. We watched these appointments unfold like a poorly scripted play. There was little we could do but endure.

Brigadier General Bajowa (rtd.) was a unique figure in the airline's history—the only army officer given the responsibility to manage Nigeria Airways. It was often viewed as an extension of the Nigerian Air Force, and many of his colleagues from the Air Force, both active and retired, found themselves in key positions within the airline.

Looking back, the state of Nigeria Airways mirrored the nation's struggles, both in governance and in its aspirations. What was once a symbol of national pride had, over time, become another casualty of mismanagement and political influence.

CHAPTER TWO

WHAT MADE NIGERIA AIRWAYS LTD DIFFERENT FROM OTHER FEDERAL OR STATE PARASTATALS OR CORPORATIONS

I REMEMBER THE intricate web of federal ministries, each one managing a complex array of agencies that carried out specific functions tied to their overarching goals. To make supervision more effective, these agencies often operated under independent management teams, easing the direct oversight by the minister. These parastatals, as we called them, or even corporations, were owned and partially managed by the Federal Ministry or by State Commissioners, depending on the case. For the ones whose services or products were deemed essential to the government, like some of the key corporations, their management was sometimes elevated to the cabinet office level. This ensured that their operations, capital investments, infrastructure, and equipment were all meticulously maintained by the government.

Among these, the Central Bank of Nigeria (CBN) held a unique position. As the apex financial governing body of the nation, its operations were critical, and while its buildings and assets were owned by the Federal Government, the Federal Ministry of Finance often managed it, albeit temporarily. The Nigeria International Telecommunications Ltd. (NITEL) was another parastatal that mirrored the operations of British Communications in almost every way. NITEL was responsible for approving or recommending any telephone companies aspiring to operate within Nigeria, ultimately reporting to the Federal Ministry of Communications, which oversaw its operations and ensured annual reports were sent directly to the government's seat of power.

There were many others of note—the Nigeria Ports Authority (NPA), the Nigeria Shipping Line (NSL), and the Nigeria National Supply Company (NNSC). The latter once played a pivotal role as the government's arm for importing and distributing essential commodities to the people of Nigeria. But as times changed, NNSC was phased out, and no longer required in the same way as before.

Then there was the Nigerian Petroleum Corporation (NNPC), the true "goose that laid the golden egg" for the nation. It controlled the exploitation and sale of Nigerian crude oil in the international markets, earning valuable foreign currency for the government. The significance of the NNPC in shaping the nation's economy was undeniable.

However, one parastatal that stood out for its unique goals was Nigeria Airways Limited. Unlike the others, the Federal Government envisioned Nigeria Airways as a self-financing entity.

The aim was for the airline to purchase its equipment, including aircraft, from its revenues. It was born out of the former West African Airways Corporation (WAAC), with the addition of "Limited" in its name to indicate the government's intention to limit its financial obligations. Still, the airline served as the national carrier, and the government could not fully remove its hand from its operations. Especially when it came to large expenditures, like the purchase of a passenger aircraft, which could cost around $85 million. While payments were not often made in full upfront, a substantial deposit had to be made to show serious intent.

The government had no choice but to back the airline financially. After all, in times of emergency—be it war, political negotiation, or national crises—the airline was a crucial asset. It was not just about flying passengers; Nigeria Airways was a tool of statecraft, conveying troops, politicians, goods, and other essentials within Nigeria and to foreign nations. The Federal Government needed to keep its influence over the airline, ensuring it remained a vital instrument in its arsenal for both domestic and international affairs.

I once had a conversation with a very senior Captain at the club one evening. Over drinks, he told me about his days in active service with the airline. He mentioned how the government often mandated him to carry out secretive flights to various African capitals, transporting Heads of State for high-level bilateral meetings with Nigeria's Head of State. The nature of these trips was always sensitive—matters of national importance—and after the meetings, he would fly them back overnight. Occasionally, government officials would also be rushed off on emergency errands, tasked with resolving diplomatic issues that were vital to Nigeria's or Africa's interests. Most of these missions were top secret, organised under the strictest confidentiality, with orders coming directly from the government.

But there was a catch, Nigeria Airways often bore the brunt of these arrangements. Sometimes, the government delayed reimbursement, or worse, did not pay at all. It is something I wonder about, even now: was the airline ever properly compensated for the services rendered? It is a question for a deeper exploration later in this book.

At that time, the Nigerian Air Force had already been established, but it did not have the kind of military jets that could be discreetly dispatched for such sensitive national assignments. Besides, the sight of a military jet might raise too many questions and arouse suspicion. Civilian passenger planes like those of Nigeria Airways, however, moved unnoticed, their presence looked ordinary and unquestioned. Of course, the government did use military jets when necessary, such as when they ousted the President of Gambia, but for most diplomatic missions, it was the commercial planes that quietly flew under the radar.

Leadership at Nigeria Airways was another story altogether. Anyone with connections, someone in the corridors of power or who had the ear of the president or Minister of Aviation, could find themselves appointed as Managing Director or CEO of the airline, regardless of experience or qualifications. It was common knowledge. I recall one instance in particular, during a course closing lecture given by Alhaji (Dr) Maigida, a former Director of Personnel. He showed us a printed list of the airline's objectives.

WHAT MADE NIGERIA AIRWAYS LTD DIFFERENT

These were lofty goals, filled with promise. Yet, as I had seen firsthand, the airline did not have the backing or autonomy to execute them properly. External interference constantly got in the way.

The Federal Civil Aviation Authority (FCAA) was supposed to be a sister organisation to Nigeria Airways, a partnership where both could thrive by working together on matters related to AFRAA, ICAO, and IATA policies. But in reality, the FCAA turned out to be one of the airline's biggest obstacles. Corruption and nepotism had rotted the agency from the inside. Many of the top officials at FCAA had once worked for Nigeria Airways—they were former employees who had been sacked, retrenched, or retired. Yet, these same individuals had returned to power, promoted without so much as a check of their records, and their new positions allowed them to undermine the very airline they once served.

The manipulation was blatant. Whenever the daily flight schedules were drawn up, Nigeria Airways flights were deliberately listed at the bottom. Private airlines, with their wealth and connections, managed to secure the coveted early departures to high-demand destinations like Abuja, Kano, and Port-Harcourt. It was a ruthless game of influence, where personal relationships determined priority over fairness. I always thought that, in a just world, the lucrative routes should be rotated among the airlines, ensuring everyone had an equal opportunity. But fairness was seldom on display.

Appointments to the leadership of Nigeria Airways were similarly dictated by favouritism. Time and time again, people were chosen for roles not because of their qualifications but because someone in power decided to do them a favour. Nigeria Airways became a playground for political appointees, with little regard for the airline's long-term health or future. Over the years, we saw an endless procession of managing directors—some from the Nigerian Air Force, others from unrelated sectors. Air Vice Marshalls Bello, Anthony Okpere, Group Captain Bernard Banfa, and from the Nigerian Army was Brigadier Olu Bajowa (retired).

CHAPTER THREE

THE OBJECTIVES AND GOVERNMENT USES OF NIGERIA AIRWAYS

When Nigeria Airways Ltd. was first established by the Federal Government of Nigeria, its mission was clear: to provide efficient passenger and cargo services across domestic airports and to connect Nigeria to the world through international flights. However, looking back, I realise that the naming of the airline as a "Limited" company created a layer of complexity. Had it been called Nigeria Airways Corporation; its purpose might have been easier to define and more straightforward to manage. But adding "Limited Liability" to its name opened the door to broader commercial implications, which shaped its operations in unexpected ways.

You see, corporations owned by the government are usually financed and managed by the state. In contrast, limited liability companies, like Nigeria Airways, were expected by law to either be self-sustaining or depend on private shareholders or the stock market to finance their operations and growth. Unlike typical corporations relying on government funding, Nigeria Airways sent its annual budget to the Minister of Aviation not for approval, but merely for notification. It was rare for the Ministry to intervene, but they had the authority to offer advice if the airline's budget strayed too far from the national interest.

International flights for Nigeria Airways were governed by bilateral agreements. These agreements, the result of intense negotiations involving the airline, the Federal Civil Aviation Authority (FCCA), and overseen by the Ministry of Aviation, laid out the terms by which Nigeria Airways could operate in foreign skies. Each agreement specified which countries the airline could fly to, how often, and which airports they could land at. Even the smallest details—arrival and departure times, the amount of time the plane could remain on the ground, and strict schedules—were meticulously outlined. Any deviation from these agreements could disrupt not just Nigeria Airways' schedule, but the entire network of flights, leading to hefty fines for non-compliance.

These agreements also covered the fees that countries would charge each other for the use of their airspace. When foreign airlines used Nigeria's airspace, they paid the FCCA, the designated authority for the Federal Republic of Nigeria. However, bilateral agreements were not always honoured. For various reasons—whether due to a lack of aircraft, unprofitable routes, or the risk of hijackings—some routes that were initially agreed upon were never operated. In such cases, Nigeria Airways could subcontract the route to another airline, with agreed charges paid to Nigeria Airways, though not directly. Payments were made in foreign currency to the FCCA, who were responsible for handling the funds on behalf of the national carrier.

THE OBJECTIVES AND GOVERNMENT USES OF NIGERIA AIRWAYS

The unfortunate truth, though, is that records show these payments rarely made their way back to Nigeria Airways from their sister corporation. It was a troubling flaw in the system, one that I often reflect on when thinking about the challenges we faced during those years.

Gone are the days when the Ministry of Aviation held immense influence over Nigeria Airways. Acting as the government's representative, their power was felt in every corner of the airline's operations. No decision could be made without their oversight, and this was particularly true for day-to-day activities. Among these influences are:

- With the appointment of the managing director or Chief Executive Officer, the Ministry had to approve any candidate before the President made the final announcement.
- Every executive director of the airline, whether promoted internally or hired from outside, was similarly chosen with the Ministry's recommendation before reaching the Presidency.
- Even something as routine as setting flight ticket prices required the Ministry's stamp of approval.

This close oversight often led to tension, and I recall a time when the entire board of executive directors was relieved of their duties, en-mass, due to disagreements. A sole administrator was swiftly appointed to manage the airline on an interim basis. Purchasing aircraft was no different; Nigeria Airways could only proceed with such transactions if the Ministry guaranteed the purchase. Without their approval, the planes would remain grounded.

This level of control was not unique to Nigeria Airways. Every organisation, no matter its size, whether social or commercial, must have clearly defined objectives and the means to achieve them. Even something as simple as a family meeting requires structure to avoid chaos. Without clear goals, we risk moving aimlessly, like wind that brings no good.

Looking back, I often think that had Nigeria Airways been named Nigeria Airways Corporation, its objectives might have been easier to define. We would not have had to guess how to achieve its goals. The airline was founded on the model of the British Overseas Airways Corporation (BOAC), which was state-financed and served as the air connection to Britain's colonies. Yet, unlike BOAC, Nigeria Airways was established as a limited liability company, meaning it was supposed to be self-financing and self-administered.

That term, "limited liability," changed everything. Unlike corporations owned and financed by the government, Nigeria Airways was expected to rely on its shareholders or the stock exchange for capital. Instead of depending on government handouts, it was supposed to stand on its own, raising funds through the sale of shares for its future projects and expansion.

International negotiations were another critical area overseen by the Ministry of Aviation. Bilateral agreements determined which countries Nigerian planes could fly to, which airports they could land at, and how long they could stay. These agreements were meticulously negotiated by experienced ministry officials, ensuring Nigeria Airways could operate smoothly abroad. Failure to comply with these agreements, whether arriving late or overstaying, resulted in fines from foreign airport authorities, adding further complications to an already challenging industry.

In addition, the International Air Transport Authority (IATA) allowed countries to levy charges for the use of their airspace. In Nigeria, it was the Federal Civil Aviation Authority that collected these dues from foreign airlines. With a limited fleet and insufficient passengers or cargo to maximise the airline's potential, Nigeria Airways often reallocated or swapped its international route agreements. This allowed private or national carriers to use these routes, though they had to pay the internationally approved rate, with the Federal Ministry of Aviation overseeing such payments.

These were the challenges we faced, day in and day out, as we tried to navigate the complexities of running a national airline under the heavy hand of government supervision. There were days when Nigeria Airways stood tall among the global giants of aviation. As a key member of the International Air Transport Association (IATA), headquartered in Switzerland, we played a significant role in regulating airspace worldwide. The IATA assigned us the flight code "WT" to distinguish Nigeria Airways from other operators, wherever our planes flew. We were also part of the International Civil Aviation Organisation (ICAO), based in Montreal, Canada, which gave Nigeria Airways the code "NIS." The Federal Ministry of Aviation, acting as the supervisory power of the Nigerian government, carefully reviewed, amended, and eventually approved Nigeria Airways' objectives.

As a government establishment, Nigeria Airways was not just a commercial venture; it is often found serving political ends. Its aircraft were occasionally used for secret missions, transporting African heads of state and their entourages to high-profile meetings. These clandestine flights never appeared on public schedules or airport records. Even the pilots and crew were kept in the dark until moments before take-off. I can still remember the sense of urgency and the weight of responsibility when such orders came through, shrouded in secrecy.

The pilots and cabin crews were held to the highest standards, undergoing rigorous training to ensure they were fit to fly the fleet. The training served two purposes: one, to keep the staff updated with the latest technologies in aviation; and two, to create avenues for promotion, allowing pilots to move up from smaller aircraft to larger ones. Safety was paramount to Nigeria Airways, and it prided itself on maintaining accident-free operations. The reputation of an airline, after all, is built on its safety record, and any mishap could spell disaster for passenger confidence.

The engineering department was just as vital. Nigeria Airways had the expertise to handle most repairs and maintenance at their hangar, including the regular A, B, and C checks necessary for each aircraft. The more extensive D checks, which required completely stripping the plane, were often done at licensed hangars abroad, such as Air Lingus in Ireland. The maintenance protocols were thorough, ensuring their planes were always in top condition.

Then there was the catering service, which was supposed to provide meals of international standard on both domestic and international flights. There was a time when two unions, the National Union of Air Travel Service Employees (NUATSE) and the Air Transport Staff Senior Service of Aviation of Nigeria

THE OBJECTIVES AND GOVERNMENT USES OF NIGERIA AIRWAYS

(ATTSSSAN), proposed upgrading the catering services. Their vision was for Nigeria Airways to become a hub for foreign airlines to source in-flight meals for their return trips. Sadly, this proposal never came to fruition. Whether it was due to internal politics or self-interest, the idea was dismissed before it could even be considered.

Ground support was another area where Nigeria Airways could have excelled, offering services to smaller, private airlines and even foreign operators. But again, corruption and self-serving interests blocked these initiatives. Profitable proposals were often buried if they did not benefit those in power. One glaring example was the Hajj operations. Private contractors were assigned the task of flying pilgrims to Mecca, but when they failed to complete the job, it was Nigeria Airways that was called upon to finish the task—without compensation. I vividly recall the chaos when thousands of pilgrims returned home, but their luggage was left stranded in Saudi Arabia. The Presidency would step in, instructing the Minister of Aviation to give a matching order to Nigeria Airways to carry out cargo flights, often making up to ten trips just to retrieve the luggage, all at the institution's expense.

International routes were another source of revenue—or they should have been. Nigeria Airways had bilateral agreements with several countries, but due to insufficient passenger numbers, it subcontracted many of these routes to other airlines. These airlines paid Nigeria Airways in foreign currency, and over the years, the amount accumulated to millions of dollars. Yet, by the time Nigeria Airways was liquidated in 2003, no one could account for where all that money had gone. It was a mystery, shrouded in the same secrecy that had defined so much of Nigeria Airways operations.

Housing for the staff was another priority. The entire Government Reserved Area (GRA) in Ikeja was once Nigeria Airways property, reserved for pilots and essential staff. This was necessary because of the long, unpredictable hours they worked, and the need for the team to be available at a moment's notice. The airline even acquired houses at Ipaja Housing Estate and land at Ayoboland, with plans to develop it into a housing estate for staff. But what became of these properties? That story, too, lies beyond the scope of this narrative.

CHAPTER FOUR

THE SUPERVISORY OF THE FEDERAL MINISTRY OF AVIATION OVER NIGERIA AIRWAYS

WHEN I REFLECT on the political outlook of Nigeria, I cannot help but notice how things shift dramatically whenever a new administration takes office, following a presidential election. It is a phenomenon I have witnessed multiple times. The transition of power does not merely affect policies; it shakes up the entire structure of governance, starting with the appointment of ministers. These appointments are heavily influenced by the key supporters and campaigners—the recognised financiers of the ruling party. Some refer to these individuals as political cabals, but in my view, they serve as the eyes and breathing nerves of the newly elected president, ensuring their influence is felt in the shaping of the ministerial structure.

These powerful backers help determine who becomes a minister, how many federal ministers will serve, and whose names are sent to the Senate for screening and confirmation. They even have a say in which ministry these ministers will supervise. Over time, I have seen how the names and portfolios of ministries in Nigeria change, often reflecting the vision of the sitting president.

For example, before the presidency of Muhammadu Buhari, there was once a Federal Ministry of Aviation. But when Buhari assumed office, he merged it with the Ministry of Transportation, renaming it the Federal Ministry of Transportation. Under this new structure, there was a junior minister assigned to aviation. However, after Buhari handed over power to President Bola Ahmed Tinubu on May 29, 2023, the name was quickly reverted to the Federal Ministry of Aviation and Aerospace.

The role of the Minister of Aviation is critical. Whoever occupies that position is responsible for regulating air travel and aviation services in the country, except for matters relating to the Nigerian Air Force. The minister holds the power to shape policies, not just for government-owned enterprises but also for private-sector players. They have to keep the president informed on matters concerning aviation and address any queries or challenges that may arise. In the event of an aircraft accident, the minister can set up a committee to investigate the cause and prevent future occurrences. They must also inform the public, either directly or through a spokesperson.

I remember a recent case that caught the nation's attention—a private airline had leased an aircraft from another airline, and it was operated by the crew of the lender. The flight, scheduled for Abuja, was mistakenly directed to Asaba due to an error with the flight manifest. Whether it was the fault of the foreign pilot, who may have misread the document, or the fault of the person who issued the wrong manifest, the incident sparked an investigation. Nigerians eagerly await the outcome, hoping that the inquiry will expose the truth and prevent similar mistakes in the future.

Unfortunately, not all ministers appointed to this prestigious position have left a positive legacy. Some have faced heavy criticism for their shambolic tenure, leaving a bad taste in the mouths of Nigerians. One of the enduring challenges Nigeria faces, both at home and abroad, is corruption and money laundering. Corruption is deeply rooted in our system, and it is one of the reasons why Nigerians are often met with suspicion when they present their green passports at foreign airports. Border control officials, aware of the country's reputation, scrutinise every Nigerian traveller as if to say, "Be thorough; do not make assumptions."

In Nigeria, just like in any other country, there are good people and bad. But when one is appointed to such a high political office, the eyes of the world—not just Nigerians—are watching. The responsibility is immense, and the stakes are high. Those entrusted with these roles must rise to the occasion, for their actions reflect not only on themselves but on the nation as a whole.

As I reflect on the tumultuous events during President Tinubu's administration, I remember the buzz that filled the air when a new wave of young men and women were nominated for ministerial appointments. Their names had been sent to the Senate for screening after thorough background checks, and the anticipation was palpable. However, what unfolded during the live televised session was nothing short of a farce.

One candidate found himself at the centre of controversy when it was revealed that he had once voiced criticism against the country after being denied a satisfactory outcome for his application. Despite meeting all the necessary criteria, he faced relentless scrutiny. Ironically, none of the senators could effectively challenge the validity of his grievances regarding the unjust denial of his rightful opportunity.

The situation grew more absurd as it became clear that some government officials were discontented with the young man's refusal to engage in corrupt practices. Instead of facilitating his rightful appointment, they deferred his case repeatedly, like a child caught in a frustrating game of yo-yo. Frustrated by this treatment, he spoke out, and his honesty was branded as unpatriotic. Thankfully, the President of the Senate intervened, and his name was eventually added to the approved candidates.

Once in office, the young man made headlines by revolutionising the Immigration Service of Nigeria, processing 28,000 passports in just three months. Applicants who had long awaited their documents could finally share stories of efficiency unheard of in the past. In a groundbreaking shift, passports could now be issued within 48 hours of submission, with applications handled online and delivered directly to applicants' addresses. It was as if we had stepped into another era altogether.

The history of Nigeria's ministers of aviation since 1960 is marked by figures who often left a bitter taste in our mouths. Stella Oduah's tenure ended in disgrace, marred by money laundering allegations from the EFCC. Then there was Femi Remi-Kayode, embroiled in a scandal for soliciting inflated bids from foreign contractors. Most recently, Senator Hadi Sirika's time in office failed to produce tangible improvements in the aviation sector.

Despite pledging the launch of Nigeria Air, a dream that had remained unfulfilled since the days of Virgin Airways, the details of this ambitious plan were shrouded in secrecy, announced not at home but during an air show in Peterborough.

As Nigerians, we are tenacious, often refusing to accept defeat even when it stares us down. Yet, our politicians seem more concerned with personal gain than the public good. The second attempt to launch Nigeria Air was particularly absurd, especially coming from someone so entrenched in government. I remember the moment the President was invited to unveil this new airline, only for the aircraft to be revealed as an Ethiopian plane, bearing an Ethiopian registration number, yet festooned with the name "Nigeria Air." Observers quickly caught on to the deception, raising questions about how much of our scarce resources had been funnelled into this ill-fated project.

History tells us of Nigeria Airways once aiding a struggling Ethiopian airline, and now, here we were, witnesses to a farcical revival that was far from the ambitious vision it purported to be. It felt as if we were trapped in a cycle of repetition, grappling with the remnants of past failures while yearning for a brighter future.

It is undeniable that former senator Hadi Sirika held an untouchable position in Nigeria's political arena. The Economic and Financial Crimes Commission (EFCC) has not disclosed any concrete details regarding their investigation of him, except to say they were looking into potential misconduct related to the project. Sirika himself expressed great satisfaction when the project finally took off, describing the journey as "a long, tedious, daunting, and difficult path."

But let us turn our attention to the heart of the matter: what role did the Ministry of Aviation play in the operation and eventual liquidation of Nigeria Airways? As the Minister of Aviation, Sirika was appointed by the President of Nigeria and was subject to Senate confirmation. During his screening, he vowed to serve the public interest, both the staff who operated the aircraft and the passengers who relied on the airline to travel safely between airports. Once his confirmation was secured, his accountability shifted almost entirely to the President. Each year, he submitted a report of his ministry's activities directly to the President, with the Senate only stepping in when national or international issues required further clarification.

In the case of Nigeria Airways, the ministry oversaw the appointment of the Board of Directors, who were supposed to manage the airline's overall operations. However, history reveals that these appointments were often influenced by the President, and many of the chosen board members were not aviation experts. They were, more often than not, politicians who had failed in previous elections, appointed to these roles as compensation for their campaign losses. These individuals did not focus on improving services, infrastructure, or the airline's finances. Instead, their primary concern was how they could personally benefit from their appointments. It was an open secret that many board members embarked on duty tours that served no real purpose other than to justify the expenditure of foreign currencies. Their "familiarisation tours" often started with visits to Nigerian airports, followed by trips to international stations where they could collect travel allowances in American dollars. For them, this was a right they felt entitled to exercise.

THE SUPERVISORY OF THE FEDERAL MINISTRY OF AVIATION

The Minister of Aviation was also responsible for liaising with the Presidency regarding the appointment of the airline's executive directors. Experience had shown that a director could be dismissed by the Minister at any moment, often without the workers ever knowing the reasons. I recall one such instance involving Dr. Maigida, a powerful director during his tenure. Military generals visited him regularly, seeking favours, yet despite his influence, he was abruptly removed from his position. With his connections, however, he soon secured a new job as a director at one of the country's top banks.

One incident from 1986 remains etched in my memory when over 3,600 staff members were retrenched. The manager responsible for coordinating the names for retrenchment, along with his selected team, never arrived at the office in the morning like everyone else. Instead, they would come in after hours, long after the regular staff had gone home for the day.

December had become synonymous with retrenchment at Nigeria Airways. While workers in other industries were advocating for promotions, wage increases, and better working conditions, the staff at Nigeria Airways lived in a state of constant dread. There was no telling who might find their name on the list. Criminal records or previous infractions had little bearing on the decision, retrenchment was simply a matter of reducing staff numbers in a given section, from, say, 30 people down to 10.

The most astonishing moment came when the manager responsible for compiling the retrenchment list was summoned to the Managing Director's office. He likely expected a handshake, a word of thanks, perhaps even a promotion to Director of

Human Resources. Instead, to everyone's shock, he was handed his letter of retrenchment. It was a deeply humiliating and dehumanising end to his service. There was no one to whom he could appeal this treatment, so he had no choice but to accept his fate.

When the new Director of Human Resources was appointed, it took many of us by surprise. He was not from the Personnel Department, as one might expect, but came from the Corporate Planning Department instead. Word soon spread that he hailed from the same state, and even the same locality, as the Chief Executive Officer of the airline. The connection was hard to overlook.

In my role as the Officer responsible for company housing and offices, I was tasked with showing him around his new office and introducing him to his staff—those who had been reassigned after the mass retrenchments. As we settled into his office, I congratulated him on his new role, but I could not help but probe, out of curiosity, about how fortunate it seemed that the Purchasing and Property Divisions had merged under the recent reorganisation. He sidestepped the question with diplomatic ease, offering no real explanation.

Seeing as we were both Yoruba men, I felt compelled to share my candid opinion, cautioning him. "All eyes will be on you," I warned. "You should be careful, and if I may suggest, always tune in to the Voice of Nigeria Radio Station at the 16:00 News."

He raised an eyebrow and asked why. I met his gaze directly, explaining with all honesty, "That's where they announce new appointments and the removal of airline directors."

From his expression, I could tell my comment did not sit well with him. But I had only told him the truth—the truth that had long been written in the history of the airline.

This was not the first time we had witnessed the influence of the Minister of Aviation. When the Nigeria Airways management unilaterally increased passenger ticket prices without consulting the ministry, it was not long before all the executive directors were removed from their positions. Andrew Agom was then appointed as the Sole Administrator of the airline, and immediately, questions arose. His appointment was not based on any clear merit or criteria; it seemed politically and tribally motivated. Such power, we knew, could not have been exercised without the backing of the highest political authorities in power.

In those days, the interplay of politics and tribalism shaped the very foundation of the airline, and appointments were often decided by forces far beyond the walls of corporate offices.

I remember the time when the Hajj operation was one of the national airline's most crucial assignments. It was a serious duty to ensure thousands of pilgrims made their sacred journey to Mecca safely. Yet, there was always a lingering sense of unease in the air, as political heavyweights constantly lobbied the government, eager to wrest control of the operation from the national airline. They wanted to take charge of conveying pilgrims to Mecca, even though most of these politicians lacked airlines or aircraft of their own to fulfil such contracts.

It became increasingly clear that the Minister, who held authority over the airline, was not innocent in this scheme. I could not shake the feeling that his actions might have been guided by directives from those higher up in the political hierarchy. But his interference went far beyond merely overseeing the Hajj operations. Time and again, he would issue orders to the airline, tasks that clearly were not in the airline's best interest.

When pilgrims set off to Mecca, they often carried only a single suitcase. But upon their return, the luggage multiplied—sometimes up to ten bags per person. Those private contractors who took over parts of the operation would hire aircraft for the first leg of the journey but, on the return, would only allow one or two bags. These left piles of luggage stranded in Jeddah. And it was always the national airline that bore the burden. The Minister would personally instruct the Chief Executive Officer to ensure that all the remaining baggage was returned to Nigeria within an unreasonable timeframe, often requiring the airline to make ten or fifteen additional trips just to ferry the luggage home—without receiving a single naira in compensation.

This was not where the corruption ended. It became common knowledge within the airline that certain individuals who were hungry for political favour would collaborate with unscrupulous staff to create false projects. These so-called property projects, designed without the management's approval or any formal public tender, were mysteriously fast-tracked. Somehow, they would always make their way to the Presidency, where a recommendation for approval would be rubber-stamped and sent back to the Minister of Aviation. From there, the Minister would forward it directly to our CEO, who had little choice but to comply. Any Managing Director who wanted to keep his job knew better than to raise objections or question these contracts.

THE SUPERVISORY OF THE FEDERAL MINISTRY OF AVIATION

The weight of these fraudulent schemes bore down on the airline. Each contract became a financial burden, and the airline was often left scrambling for funds to execute projects it neither needed nor requested. It was a painful chapter, where the interests of the national airline were sacrificed at the altar of political greed.

When I joined the airline in July, from the moment I arrived, people kept mentioning that the airline's annual budget was still awaiting approval from the Ministry. This was not just a formality. The Ministry wielded significant power—scrutinising and ratifying every detail of the budget. Because of this delay, I had no choice but to accept a position two grade levels below what my education qualified me for. In those days, if you did not have a godfather, a politician, or a General backing you, holding a signed complimentary card, you simply had to settle for whatever position was offered.

This was not just my story—many projects within the airline were left unimplemented or completely abandoned due to the endless waiting for budget approval. It was a recurring theme, a frustration that lingered in the air. I still recall when Andrew Agom was removed as the Sole Administrator of the airline. His removal had nothing to do with poor performance or bad management. No, it was a power struggle at the highest level of politics in the country. Rumour had it that the Presidency had plans to reward someone who had been generous to them during his time as a high-ranking officer in the Nigerian Army. His private business was on the decline, and the solution seemed to be appointing him to head the airline.

That decision nearly caused an uproar within the Nigerian Air Force (NAF). Middle-ranking officers could not understand why a Nigerian Army officer was being appointed to lead Nigeria Airways—a role they believed should belong to someone from the NAF, which had long seen the airline as an extension of their institution. The tension was palpable. Eventually, a compromise was reached. A retired Air Vice-Marshal, Bello, was appointed as the chairman of the Presidential Task Force overseeing the airline, while the former Sole Administrator—a retired Army officer—was made Managing Director and a member of the task force.

The airline had several bilateral routes with other countries that, due to various factors, could not operate. These routes were instead handed over to international airlines, who, in turn, paid for the rights to operate them. But even here, the bureaucracy was stifling— the Federal Civil Aviation Authority collected these fees on behalf of the airline, all under the direction of the Ministry of Aviation. It makes you wonder why the Economic and Financial Crimes Commission (EFCC) has not investigated this, especially since former staff of the airline still have not received their full pension payments. President Buhari approved payments as far back as 2018, yet the balance remains unpaid. But with the airline's liquidation, many see that chapter as closed. The documents were destroyed—the MOPOL was even ordered to burn them in front of Airways House.

Yet, for all the frustrations of the common workers, there was another world of privilege that flourished within the airline. I cannot count how many businessmen, politicians, military officers, traditional rulers, and religious leaders travelled abroad with their

THE SUPERVISORY OF THE FEDERAL MINISTRY OF AVIATION

families, all on first-class tickets they did not pay full price for. All it took was a well-placed letter to the Presidency, asking for a special rebate. The letter would go through the proper channels, from the Presidency to the Minister of Aviation, who would endorse it and pass it on to the airline's Managing Director for approval. The prices they paid were laughably low—an abuse of privilege and a clear misuse of IATA regulations, which were meant to grant special rates only to airline employees and their families.

It was a time of contradictions—privilege and frustration, opportunity and delay. And in the end, the airline's story was one of missed potential, lost to the shifting winds of politics and power.

Looking back on those times, I remember clearly the lists of names—men of wealth, fortunate enough to be in a position where they could buy aircraft for our national airline. It reminded me of what we read in the papers about Saudi Arabia, where some of the wealthiest citizens would willingly purchase aircraft for their national fleet, a gesture of pride and patriotism. But here in Nigeria, things were different. Rather than uplifting the nation from its roots, we seemed to take from the poor to fill the pockets of the rich and powerful. I could not help but reflect on the teachings of the New Testament and think if only we applied the principles of fairness, perhaps we would be in a better place. God help my country, Nigeria.

When it came to air travel, tickets were sold through a variety of channels. Travellers could walk into the booking offices that the airline had conveniently set up in most state capitals and purchase their tickets directly. Then there were agents—individuals or businesses contracted to sell tickets to the public, especially online. Within Nigeria, these agents were carefully monitored. There was a section of the Accounts Department, known as the Ticket Accounts Section, dedicated to supervising them. They would visit these agents, sometimes giving advance notice, but if there was suspicion of misconduct, an unannounced visit could be arranged. Accountability was key, or at least it was meant to be. But when it came to foreign nations, places like the UK, the USA, or Saudi Arabia, it was a different story. The Federal Ministry of Aviation had a heavy hand in selecting which agents would be appointed to sell tickets abroad. It was less about capability and more about power—a way for the ministry to assert its influence. And of course, there were stories, more than a few, about agents who simply disappeared with the airline's funds, leaving behind a financial black hole. The airline would lose vast sums of money, often in foreign currencies, and yet the ministry responsible would evade any accountability for these losses. It was a frustrating cycle, one that seemed to repeat itself, unchecked by those who held the power to stop it.

CHAPTER FIVE

EXTERNAL POWERS THAT FORMULATE POLICIES ON NIGERIA AIRWAYS

IT IS IMPORTANT to always remind ourselves that Nigeria Airways was an establishment of the Federal government of Nigeria. In those times, decisions surrounding the airline's operations and policies were determined by a select few within the corridors of power. However, in our present era of democratic governance, things would have unfolded quite differently. Today, any issues or policies related to a national entity like Nigeria Airways would first pass through the Senate and the House of Representatives. The Presidency would propose ideas, and through the legislative process, many amendments might reshape the vision before it could be implemented.

Take, for example, the recent legislation on student loans. The initial approved law was not left untouched. It was revisited, revised, and moulded by the government in consultation with student union bodies and Non-Governmental Organisations

(NGOs), all of whom had their voices heard. In the end, the legislation became a product of collaboration, tailored to meet the desires of multiple stakeholders. If Nigeria Airways were to be revived today, the appointment of a new Managing Director would undoubtedly go through a similar process. The Senate would screen any candidate before the confirmation of their role, much like the newly appointed MD of the Nigeria Airport Authority had to face such scrutiny. This kind of process ensures that the public is informed about the background and experience of the individual at the helm, and it gives them a glimpse of the promises made for the improvement of the national carrier.

We must remember that aviation is no ordinary business. It is a delicate and highly scrutinised industry, with eyes from around the world constantly monitoring its activities. A single aircraft accident could claim countless lives, both passengers and crew, and the cost of replacing a plane in monetary terms alone is staggering. Considering these factors, it is clear that the aviation industry must be governed by bodies equipped to oversee its operations on both domestic and international levels.

Nigeria Airways, like any major airline, did not exist in isolation. Its operations were intertwined with various organisations outside the country. These international bodies had significant authority over how airlines conducted their daily operations. Whether it was ensuring passenger safety or guiding relationships between countries, these organisations played a crucial role in shaping the performance and regulation of the aviation industry. The connections Nigeria Airways had to these global institutions were not just bureaucratic formalities; they were essential to

EXTERNAL POWERS THAT FORMULATE POLICIES ON NIGERIA AIRWAYS

maintaining the airline's integrity and ensuring its place on the global stage.

Looking back, I see the importance of these bodies and their influence on the aviation industry as a whole. The story of Nigeria Airways is a reminder of how deeply connected we are to the broader international aviation community and the delicate balance that must be maintained to ensure safety, trust, and collaboration in the skies.

IATA:

As I reflect on my career in aviation, one of the most influential organisations I encountered was the International Air Transport Association (IATA). This association, established in 1945, became a powerful force in the aviation industry, safeguarding both airlines and passengers across the globe. It has long been considered a neutral entity, separate from the complexities of world politics, which is why national governments give weight to its voice. Its policies are like crystal, clear and precise, helping shape global aviation standards.

IATA functions as the trade association for the world's airlines. It could be described as a kind of cartel, setting technical standards for more than 300 airlines in over 320 countries. One of its key duties is to organise tariff conferences—platforms where airline fares are discussed and set at reasonable levels, with operational costs and fair profit margins always in mind.

The organisation's influence is vast. With headquarters in Montreal, Canada, and executive offices in Geneva, Switzerland,

IATA's global reach is undeniable. I remember the conferences it held to regulate prices in international air travel, aiming to keep rates fair while ensuring that airlines remained profitable. One notable decision was its resolution to cap travel agents' commissions at 7% of the ticket price. This was not well received by agents, but IATA's authority prevailed.

In my years with Nigeria Airways, I saw firsthand the extent of IATA's power. In early 1987, the national airline was suspended from the IATA clearing house due to outstanding debts amounting to over $1.1 million. This meant Nigeria Airways could no longer issue tickets for flights on other IATA member airlines, a serious blow to the airline's operations. I still remember attending the AFRAA (African Airlines Association) conference in Abuja as a delegate of Nigeria Airways. These periodic meetings, held at the Federal Civil Aviation Authority in Ikeja, brought together key stakeholders from Nigeria Airways, the Federal Civil Aviation Authority, and the Nigeria Airport Authority. The President of IATA himself travelled from Canada to chair the conference. His presence underscored the importance of the event, especially as we were there to elect the next President of AFRAA.

These moments shaped not just my career, but also my understanding of the complex yet fascinating world of international aviation.

ICAO:

International Civil Aviation Organisation is a specialised agency of the United Nations that co-ordinated the principles and techniques

EXTERNAL POWERS THAT FORMULATE POLICIES ON NIGERIA AIRWAYS

of international air navigation and fostered the planning and development of international air transport to ensure safe and orderly growth. It has a council that adopts standards and recommends practices concerning air navigation that are followed by air transport safety authorities in countries signatory to the Convention on International Civil Aviation.

ICAO was established in 1944. It has helped countries to diplomatically and technically realise a uniquely rapid and dependable network of global air mobility connecting families, countries, and businesses all over the world. It has taken it seriously to promote sustainable growth and socio-economic prosperity wherever aircraft fly. ICAO training focuses on empowering current and future generations of available facilities to overcome industry challenges.

ANC:

Air Navigation Commission is the technical body of the ICAO. The body considers and recommends standards, practises, and procedures for Air Navigation Service for adoption and approval by ICAO. It provides navigation services to aircraft in the airspace or the manoeuvring area to ensure the safety and efficient passage of aircraft in their airspaces all around the world.

PASSPORT STANDARD:

This is a new introduction to the aviation industry and is already operational in developed countries, hopefully, it will come to

Nigeria during the tenure of the current Minister of Aviation Mr Kenyamo. It is one of the recommendations of ICAO and it has been published as standards for machine-readable passports. Machines readable passport machines are now installed at airports where one official can monitor and assist many people at existing immigration points by touching their passports on the machines and once the information is authentic, the gate will open for the passengers to exit.

The machine has an area where some of the information otherwise written in alphabetic characters printed in textual form is also written as strings of alphanumeric characters printed in a manner suitable for optical character recognition which enables border controllers and other law enforcement agents to process such passports more quickly without having to enter the information manually into a computer. I have gone through the described process at the London City Airport without hassle. It was an impressive and orderly manner. Some critics may object on the grounds of human employment which may decline or be reduced, people can be transferred to other departments where their service will continue to contribute to our aviation developments. I pray that during the tenure of President Tinubu in office, the minister of aviation in conjunction with the minister of Communication and Digital Economy Dr Bosun Tunji– Ojo will work together to usher a new dawn to Nigeria's tourism sector and make air travellers to enjoy modern and fast facilities that they enjoy in other countries. Secondly, what I termed as Nigeria's factor of people begging for money or bribes will not obstinate the programme and the efforts of the government in this direction.

ICAO assigns three letters of airline codes to flights to Lagos which is LOS, and to London LHR to mention a few that are knowledgeable to Nigerian travellers. ICAO maintain the standard for aircraft registration known as tail numbers including the alphanumeric codes that identify the country of registration.

AFRAA:

African Airline Association is a trade association of African countries' airlines. It was founded in Accra Ghana in 1969 and its headquarters is now in Nairobi Kenya. The primary purpose is to establish and facilitate cooperation between African airlines. AFRAA and its concept began in 1963 when some African States gained their Independence from Great Britain. It enabled any airline in Africa to share common factors such as cooperation and Data Intelligence etc. Only government-owned airlines could register to be a member then.

AFRAA hold their conference in member states every fourth year that rotates from one country to another when officials of the National Civil Aviation Authority are elected as the President of the association. Being the host of the conference in one country is not a guarantee that the hosting country will become the elected President. There are deals of politics, lobbying and trade by batter involved during the conference and election.

The President of IATA was often invited to monitor the process and announce the winner after all countries concerned had cast their votes. Other organisations attending the conference include aircraft manufacturers and service providers, consultants, insurers and aviation stakeholders. There was one such conference held in Abuja Nigeria, most of the delegates first arrived in Lagos and that allowed them to meet Nigerian Aviation top officials to discuss matters of importance before they proceeded to Abuja.

The Managing Director of the FCCA then narrowly won the election by a very close margin. The President was to hold the post for four years before another conference and another election was held in another country. The possibility of the coveted position being won by the same holder twice was impossible as the constitution of the body did not emphasise it.

WAAC:

This was West African Airways Corporation. It was jointly owned by the West African colonies of The Gambia, The Gold Coast renamed Ghana, Nigeria and Sierra Leone, the English-speaking countries of West Africa and members of the Commonwealth. It was initially operated by the British Overseas Airways Corporation (BOAC). It was dissolved in 1958 after all the stakeholder countries except Nigeria had set up their national airlines. Nigeria continued to operate it as WAAC which was later renamed as Nigeria Airways and became the flag bearer for Nigeria. Most of the infrastructures Nigeria Airways was known for and enjoyed during its operational years were established step by step from the BOAC years to the WAAC regime then finally to Nigeria Airways. The Airways House was constructed and most of the facilities installed are typical points of reference. The maintenance and Engineering workshop was a tourist attraction up to the time the airline was wickedly and maliciously liquidated in 2003. The structures at Obi Village particularly the White House which housed the Flight Operations, Marketing and Telecommunication were efforts of the WAAC.

Before the dwindling of Nigeria Airways, there were records that some African airlines brought their aircraft to the maintenance and Engineering of the airline for different types of checks because their airline did not have the manpower, technological knowledge, and facilities to carry out the operation to the approval of ICAO and IATA. Those infrastructures were deliberately and for reasons beyond the imagination of justice, equity and morality cannot be handed over to Arik Air. Unfortunately, we are a nation who do not question our political leaders to make them account for their actions.

CHAPTER SIX

EXTERNAL INFLUENCES WITHIN NIGERIA

IN THE ANNALS of Nigerian aviation history, Nigeria Airways Limited stood not as an independent entity but as a crucial part of a broader network of organisations. Its operations were inextricably linked to various bodies, some with noble intentions, others driven by less transparent motives, each influencing the nation's aviation activities in complex ways. Among these organisations, some shared a common origin within the same Ministry of Aviation, an entity that had once been part of the larger Federal Ministry of Transportation and Aviation before being separated into its ministry.

These affiliated bodies, known as parastatals, played a pivotal role in shaping the fortunes of Nigeria Airways. One of the most significant was the Federal Civil Aviation Authority (FCAA), a governing body whose regulations and decisions directly impacted the airline's day-to-day operations. Over time, the FCAA underwent its transformation, evolving into what we now recognize as the Nigeria Civil Aviation Authority (NCAA). This relationship between Nigeria Airways and the regulatory authority was one of both cooperation and control, a dynamic that would come to define the airline's trajectory in the shifting landscape of Nigerian aviation.

FCAA:

In the early years of Nigeria's aviation industry, a powerful entity emerged that would shape the trajectory of air travel in the country: the Federal Civil Aviation Authority (FCAA). Created as a regulatory body, the FCAA was entrusted with the delicate task of overseeing aviation safety and implementing government policies to ensure that the skies over Nigeria were secure. It was granted the power to regulate the industry independently, free from political interference—a responsibility that required impartiality and integrity. Yet, despite its mandate, the relationship between the FCAA and Nigeria Airways, the national carrier, was far from harmonious.

Nigeria Airways and the Nigeria Civil Aviation Authority (NCAA), which operated under the FCAA, were often viewed as twin sisters, entities meant to work in tandem for the nation's benefit. However, the NCAA's heavy-handed use of its regulatory authority over Nigeria Airways often bred tension. Meetings that were meant to foster cooperation between various aviation stakeholders, such as the Nigeria Airport Authority (NAA) and the Nigerian Aviation Handling Company (NAHCO), frequently became fraught with challenges. I remember attending many management meetings on behalf of Nigeria Airways at the FCAA's headquarters, tucked behind the Nigeria Airport Authority offices at Ikeja Airport. These meetings, often attended by delegates from different aviation bodies and sometimes even the Ministry of Aviation, were intended to address matters of common interest—issues that affected the entire aviation sector.

One such instance of collaboration was during the preparations for the African Airlines Association (AFRAA) conference in Abuja. The FCAA coordinated regular meetings, assigning specific tasks to officials from each aviation parastatal to ensure the conference ran smoothly. There was also an incident involving the discovery of a parcel of Indian hemp on a Nigeria Airways flight bound for West Africa. In that case, the FCAA and Nigeria Airways worked together to investigate the matter thoroughly, submitting a joint report to the Minister of Aviation.

Yet, beneath this veneer of cooperation, the FCAA wielded its influence in ways that ultimately undermined Nigeria Airways. One of the most significant areas of contention was the FCAA's control over the publication of daily flight schedules for both domestic and international routes. This power was exercised in ways that crippled Nigeria Airways, favouring private airlines that had recently been liberated to operate domestically.

In the early days of deregulation, Nigeria Airways found itself in fierce competition with these new entrants—names like Med-View, ADC, Kabo, and Sky Power Express—airlines that sprang up seemingly overnight. The FCAA, instead of maintaining a level playing field, began favouring these private airlines, often to the detriment of the national carrier. This bias was most evident in the scheduling of early morning flights, which were highly coveted by Nigerian travellers. Businesspeople, in particular, preferred these early flights so they could attend to matters in cities like Abuja, Kano, Kaduna, or Port Harcourt, and still return home the same day.

Anyone familiar with the chaotic scene at Murtala Muhammed Airport in the morning would remember how desperate travellers became to catch these early flights. I have witnessed countless scenes of businessmen and women, bags in hand, running frantically through the terminal, determined not to miss their flights. But Nigeria Airways, which should have benefited from this demand, found itself sidelined as the FCAA skewed the flight schedules in favour of its competitors.

In retrospect, the actions of the FCAA during this period cast a long shadow over Nigeria Airways, contributing to its eventual decline. What should have been a partnership between the regulatory authority and national carrier became a bitter struggle, with Nigeria Airways, the once-proud symbol of Nigerian aviation, left to bear the brunt of decisions made in boardrooms far removed from the realities of the industry. The FCAA's actions, driven by interests that remain difficult to comprehend, inflicted wounds from which Nigeria Airways would never recover.

In those days, the scene at Nigeria's airports was nothing short of chaotic. Passengers swarmed ticket counters, bribing agents and jostling for space. It wasn't uncommon to see travellers sprinting towards their flights as if they were at a bustling bus station like Oshodi or Julius Berger car park. Some even balanced their luggage on their heads, desperate to make the earliest queues. Nigeria Airways, once a symbol of national pride, had become infamous for being the last in line on domestic flight schedules. Day after day, the same pattern unfolded: by 11 a.m., the airline's planes were still grounded, waiting for their chance to take off from Ikeja, while private airlines had already completed round trips to Lagos.

This pattern of delays had serious consequences. Nigeria Airways, once trusted by its customers, began to lose them to swifter, more efficient competitors. Frustrated passengers, businessmen shipping goods, and professionals with urgent transactions at the political capital, Abuja, found the national carrier's persistent tardiness unacceptable. Time was money, and Nigeria Airways was wasting both.

Rumours swirled around the industry. Med-View Airlines, it was said, was owned by a former Nigeria Airways pilot. Likewise, Kabo Airlines was rumoured to be the creation of an ex-cabin crew member. Both supposedly had friends in high places within the Federal Civil Aviation Authority (FCAA), ensuring their flights were given priority over Nigeria Airways. Some whispered that retired captains from the national carrier, now holding influential positions at the FCAA, were quietly exacting revenge on their former employer by sabotaging flight schedules.

The real question on everyone's lips, from the public to the airline's low-level staff, was this: What were Nigeria Airways' executives doing about the chronic delays? Did the managing directors and operations executives not know, or did they simply turn a blind eye? Perhaps their hands were tied by restrictive contracts that prevented them from challenging the FCAA or involving the Minister of Aviation in domestic flight scheduling issues. Whatever the case, it seemed clear that the leadership of Nigeria Airways was failing to confront the problem head-on.

Had the managing director of Nigeria Airways raised his concerns with his counterpart at the FCAA? Had he appealed to the Minister of Aviation, voicing the frustrations of his passengers and employees? It appeared not. And so, private airlines continued to rise, benefiting from favourable treatment, while the national carrier languished. It was a missed opportunity, one that would haunt the airline for years to come.

NAA:

The executive duties allocated to the Nigeria Airports Authority (NAA) to create, develop and maintain the government-owned and operated airports in Nigeria are as follows:

1. Tarmac infrastructure improvement, and flight aid equipment improvement.
2. Aircraft documentation and airworthiness to be made more stringent
3. Aircraft departure time-table to be made rotational to give every airline the opportunity to benefit from early morning rush to Abuja, Kano and Port-Harcourt should not be an exclusive right of a few favoured airlines
4. Registration of companies to participate as airline operators should not be politicised.

Nigeria Airways was linked to the NAA now rebranded as Federal Airports Authority of Nigeria (FAAN) by sharing office locality and at airports they provide the national airlines spaces and offices to be used. While Nigeria Airways has its ground operation and equipment, the FAAN supplement in case of breakdown. One specific area the FAAN was linked with Nigeria Airways was through the joint members of their workers through the trade Union activities called Nigerian Union of Air Transport Services (NUATSE) and later established was the Air Transport Senior Staff Association of Nigeria (ATSSAN). When it was realised that NAA was not sincere in remittance of their union dues to the central body, the executive body decided to establish a separate union for the senior staff and leave the NUATSE for the Junior staff. There was acrimony as some directors in Human Resources of the airline were against the new registration by telling the executive members of the union why they had not informed them before the registration. They showed their biased leaning by supporting one group against the other and they even tried to block the union deductions of the staff from being paid to ATTSSSAN. Legendary Femi Falana had to be invited by the union officials to meet the Controller and the Director in the Human Resources of Nigeria Airways to remind them of the provisions of the Labour Law regulations stated on recognition of trade union movements.

NAHCO:

This is the Nigeria Aviation Handling Company. It was a Nigerian Air Transportation service company that offered ground handling services particularly cargo handling power distribution and fuelling for Nigeria's Air transport industry. NAHCO handled cargo flight delivery on arrival at any Nigerian airport. To foreign airlines, NAHCO offers aircraft, passenger, crew transportation and aviation training services.

The occasional complaints Nigeria Airways may have could be in the area of delay in evacuating the cargo in the aircraft as it might have been rescheduled for another flight. The effect of NAA on Nigeria Airways was very minimal

CHAPTER SEVEN

TO BECOME AN AVIATION PILOT

IN THE DAYS when one had the fortune of being associated with a commercial aviation pilot, whether as a co-worker in Personnel, Finance, Marketing, or Ground Operations at Nigeria Airways, you could not help but admire them. Perhaps you would even dream that a sibling or child would follow in their remarkable footsteps. Pilots carried a distinct air of professionalism that set them apart from the rest of the aviation workforce.

Let us begin with their uniforms—an unmistakable symbol of their standing. Whether it was the trousers, the shirts, the jackets, or the coat, each piece was customary, polished, and pristine. The cap, adorned with the airline's logo, was a spectacle in itself, instantly noticeable and commanding respect. Pilots seemed to have an inherent mastery of dressing, their uniforms tailored to perfection no matter their body type—whether they were short, tall, slim, or stout. Once dressed, they appeared as if they were destined for a fashion runway, exuding sharpness and sophistication. Their black trousers, often crafted from the finest French or Italian fabrics, were either custom-made or meticulously tailored to fit with precision. A pilot's appearance was more than just professional; it was an embodiment of elegance.

The allure of the profession went beyond their sharp attire. Even junior officers, who flew mostly local routes, enjoyed salaries and allowances that far exceeded those of high-ranking government officials. Some would argue that the high compensation was justified by the immense risks associated with the job. The weight of responsibility on a pilot's shoulders was staggering—any technical malfunction, human error, or health issue could lead to catastrophic consequences. The lives of hundreds of passengers, crew members, and fellow pilots depended on their expertise. Such high stakes might explain why pilots were known to embrace life with a sense of freedom and extravagance.

At Murtala Mohammed International Airport (MMA) in Ikeja, where I spent much time in the 1980s and 1990s, pilots were easily recognized by the luxury cars they drove. Among the best-designed and most beautiful cars in the staff parking lot, you could be sure the finest belonged to either Nigerian Air Force officers or commercial pilots.

When a commercial pilot was promoted to a higher rank, it often meant a transfer to bigger aircraft such as the Boeing 707, DC-10, Airbus, or 747, which came with the opportunity to travel internationally. Joining the prestigious club of international pilots opened doors to numerous benefits. Their landing and take-off allowances increased proportionately, and they were entitled to overnight allowances whether they stayed in a foreign country or not, as long as they were on active flight duty.

Back in those days, there was a common game pilots played. Upon arriving at a station, often in a West African country, they would call the station manager and test whether he was willing to "play the game." If the station manager was not cooperative—perhaps unwilling to offer overnight allowances or five-star hotel accommodations—the pilots would employ deliberate delay tactics, ensuring the cost of keeping them around rose significantly. A wise station manager knew it was better to comply than to incur these added expenses, which included parking fees, handling charges, and luxurious hotel stays.

The life of a pilot, with all its perks and privileges, was indeed something to aspire to—a lifestyle that combined professionalism, adventure, and a touch of glamour.

Whenever there is a social party, if the celebrant has two or three pilots in attendance either as friends or colleagues at work, you will ensure that everything practicable is made available for them to be special guests on your special occasion be it a wedding, final burial, or coronation (Iwuye) ceremony. There was once a socialite pilot whom I knew so much, that I would like to use him as a demonstration of what I am trying to illustrate. Captain Z, as I would like to refer to him on this page is a party animal to the core. You need to convince him before he can attend your party of the class of the people that would be in attendance, the name of the musician that will entertain people on the day. But once he gives his words of consent, you can be assured that he will turn up with his entourage of eminent personalities. He has a taste for wine and whenever he goes out, he takes some bottles of them with him, his own specified drink in a tray accompanied by the drinking glass he is going to use. When he stands up to dance with the celebrant, the musician ignores others in attendance and concentrates on him because he is sure of what he is going to be sprayed with dollars. Money in Naira and Dollars counts.

How does one become a flying pilot? There is only one Nigerian Aviation School situated in Zaria that serves the length and breadth of the country to fill up this profession. This is the institution that trains their enrolled students the basic civil aviation training on their way to becoming a civil aviation aircraft pilot. As I said the school teaches all the requirements both theoretical and practical and sets up the examinations of competence which must meet the standard set down by the International Air Transport Aviation.

The Nigerian Civil Aviation School has a prospectus which informs people or candidates who intend to follow the profession, of the basic subjects that are required as a platform for applying to the school for admission such as subjects in mathematics and science subjects. Because of the stringent of the profession, any applicant must possess the West African Examination Council or GCE Ordinary Level in relevant subjects such as Mathematics, Physics, Chemistry, Geography, and others as an additional bonus. Fees-wise, it is very expensive and could cost as much as over one million in local currency.

Ironically, the course is very tough to the extent that less than 25 per cent of admitted candidates completed the course. The theoretical classroom works were flexible and proficiency level or pass marks were not rigidly fixed. When it comes to practical training, texts and examinations there have been strict principles of little variations from scoring 100 per cent. The IATA regulations had set a very high level standard, on which examiners must base their pass marks. Students in some practical subjects were tested thrice, marks scored were added together and once a student scored below 98 per cent on average, that student failed the text. There is a provision for repeat and when every candidate considers the tuition fees and accommodation fees; every candidate needs to be extremely serious as repetition does not support the quality of future pilots required by the airline industry in Nigeria.

Nigeria has a Nigerian College of Aviation Technology formerly known as the Nigerian Civil Aviation Training Centre. It is situated in the township of Zaria. The Centre was established in 1964. The College has four schools in the same vicinity and they are as follows:

1. The Flying School
2. The Aircraft Maintenance Engineering School.
3. The Air Traffic Service Communications School
4. The Aeronautical Telecommunication Engineering School.

The vision of the College was to maintain the prestigious position of the foremost aviation training institution In Africa and be among the best in the world. Like a profit or rented company, the College has a mission which guides it to consistently provide the aviation industry with professional and other personnel through training services for safe transportation under international standards. While the objectives of the College were to conduct civil aviation training for use in flight training or airport operations and to train approved persons in the installation, maintenance and operation of technical equipment, the use of what calculated or likely to increase the margin of operational safety of civil aircraft services.

Candidates for admission into the college are required to be holders of a Senior Secondary School Certificate holder with a minimum of five credits which must include the important subjects of Mathematics, Physics, and English Language. Every candidate needs to present a certificate of medical fitness, to determine that no health problem may hinder the candidate from remaining in the air on flight. An entrance examination is conducted, and marked. Successful candidates were invited for very rigorous interviews where authentic certificates were thoroughly screened.

The courses required different fees ranging from ₦7,241,000 for a standard Pilot or payment of $64,652 for the 70 weeks of training to obtain a commercial Pilot Licence (Ground) that takes 20 weeks and costs ₦450,000. For an individual to progress from the initial pilot course to senior Pilot, one needs to update his flight training which would become the responsibility of an employer. A pilot in a flying logbook kept so judiciously as the Bible is to a pastor or Reverend in the service of a church.

Pilots in the service of the liquidated Nigeria Airways were sent abroad for further training and to update them from time to time to upgrade their knowledge and bring their expertise with modern technology from one aircraft to another aircraft. I knew some senior pilots who were ambitious to upgrade their status but because the airline was claiming a lack of funds to sponsor them, they helped themselves by disposing of some of their properties to acquire the required finance to proceed on self-sponsored training abroad to enable them to gain higher qualifications that will automatically qualify them for promotion. They have the desire to command a flight and the only chance of achieving that is to undertake the training and having a pilot licence does not automatically give anybody employment in an airline company. Once one is registered and issued a pilot licence, one needs to go through rigorous tests to be employed in the profession. There are many people with pilot licences even from the USA who could not get employment due to so many factors such as lack of attitude, test failure, and unsuitability for any ground for employment.

Nigeria Airways pilots have goodwill and reputations within the country and in International Pilot Association circles as competent and could fly anywhere in the world on the licence they hold. Among good pilots that Nigeria Airways has nurtured and further trained to a higher level, it is very important to mention some of them for posterity and record purposes. Captain Hayes was a well-reputed DC 10 on one flight when he landed the aircraft at the London Heathrow Airport the landing was so smooth and appreciated by the passengers that they all stood up on their sits and clapped for the captain of the aircraft and they were anxious to shake his hand as the appreciation of safe arrival at their departure airport. Captain Tahal on DC10 as well, Captain Akintaju, who has served Nigeria Airways in all grades of flights at odd hours on government assignments day and night, Captain Wale Oke, Captain Nnanchi who served as Deputy Managing Director under Alhaji Bature, Captain Briggs became the Minister of Aviation after the liquidation of the airline.

To conclude this chapter, it is necessary to show that all human beings were not saints. Despite all financial resources open to the Senior pilots, some of them were still in breach of their professional rules and the laid down regulations. The regulation I am referring to is very strict and is to be adhered to and implemented once a pilot is found to bring the profession into disrepute. When a pilot had an accident, let us assume a minor ground accident which does not involve the death of the pilot or that of the passengers, the ministry of aviation has a committee of investigators that will swing into investigation to reveal the causes of the accident. If it was found out to be an aircraft disfunction, the pilot will be exonerated but may be restrained before going back to piloting an aircraft.

What is most unacceptable was for a pilot to be involved in case of drug, either as a user or found to be transporting or be accessary to its distribution. There are some Nigeria Airways pilots who were discharged from the service of the airline because they were found in possession of drugs concealed in their flying bags or on their body. Most of these incidents were detected when their flights arrived in foreign countries particularly in the USA where searching was very extensive and mechanical. There was a case of a particular very senior captain on DC10 because of his good records, experience and long service with the airline, he was also appointed as a training specialist of cabin crews' courses after they have joined the airline. One day in the class of training, he was teaching his students the problems that they would face if they were cut with drug trafficking either within Nigeria or abroad and the shame such action would bring to the reputation of the airline.

On the same night, he had a flight from Lagos to London (LOS—LHR). At the Heathrow airport, the antinarcotic dog sniffed a drug in his luggage, he was asked to stand aside, searched and found with drug. He was arrested, prosecuted and imprisoned. That incident led to his service being terminated from the company. Even for those on annual leave i.e. who were not on active service at the time of detention, their commercial flight licence would be cancelled and once the incident is brought to the notice of the management, it must be reported to AITA, that pilot licence would be cancelled and he cannot be in the cockpit as a pilot for life.

The pilots are human beings, they might be pre-occupied with managing their erratic work schedules, planning their flights and conducting their pre-flight check-ups, so they can neglect their health. Due to their job description, a lot of pilots suffer from stress, fatigue, sleep deprivation and unhealthy eating habits. The pilot is to plot out a safe flight route, analyse flight plans, check the condition of the aircraft and monitor the instruments in the cockpit. Airline pilots have to cooperate with their teams to ensure that their SOPs are followed. Having good team synergy also allows for better communication and builds trust so that the airline crew can work efficiently throughout their voyage.

Despite most modern technologies built in the latest and modern aircraft to endure all kinds of incidents of weather conditions, it is the job of aircraft pilot to fly their passengers safely through thunderstorms, and strong winds, and avoid flying birds and other turbulence. Commercial pilots bear substantial responsibility for the safety of their passengers and crews. Situational awareness and ability to handle various scenarios.

Gard Aviation is a leading aviation institute that can help aspiring pilots navigate challenges and simulator training. They help to provide access to job listings, industry news and networking opportunities. They also provide continuing education and training programmes. Many Nigerian commercial pilots were trained in the United States of America and in the United Kingdom aviation industries. Most were sponsored by their families. Some were able to be granted a scholarship by the Federal government and State governments to undergo the training. Some other countries assisted in training Nigerian pilots notable ones were Israel and Egypt.

It was also on record that in the 1970s, the Federal government granted student loans to some young people to be trained in the United Kingdom so that they could take the place of the foreign pilots on Nigerian indigenous airlines. The course was given priority among many other courses.

CHAPTER EIGHT

MANAGING NIGERIA AIRWAYS LTD

THE RELATIONSHIP BETWEEN Nigeria Airways and the Federal Ministry of Aviation has always been a deeply intertwined one. As a 100% shareholder in the airline through the Federal Government, the ministry functioned as an appendage, overseeing the airline's operations and making key decisions. Empowered as an executive arm of the central government, the ministry held the authority to craft policies and make appointments that would shape the airline's future. Its role was not merely administrative; it was intended to act as a shield, safeguarding Nigeria Airways from both internal and external pressures. The ministry, by its design, was tasked with selecting individuals to form the Board of Directors for the company. Once chosen, these members wielded significant power, often immune to legal or social criticism. While democracy now allows for more open debate and scrutiny, in practice, once a minister secured presidential approval, his selections were final. The criteria for these appointments were not always rooted in expertise within the aviation industry. Over the years, board members came from diverse backgrounds: business management, accounting, engineering, and other professions, based largely on the government's approval of the minister's list.

The driving objective behind these selections was consistent: to improve Nigeria Airways and strive for profitability. The next pivotal appointment was for the Managing Director/Chief Executive Officer (MD/CEO), a decision often swayed by the government's broad powers. Over time, the selection process for the MD/CEO varied, drawing candidates from within the airline's ranks, the public service, or even the armed forces. While certain departments, such as Finance and Marketing, had never held the top position, others saw their personnel rise to the occasion. The Director of Personnel, now commonly referred to as Human Resources, once saw Alhaji Bature promoted to Managing Director, with the support of a skilled deputy, Captain Nnachi, an experienced pilot. Similarly, Flight Operations often provided a steady stream of leadership, as many senior captains balanced the dual roles of managing director and maintaining flight schedules. Among them were notable figures such as Captains Tahal, Atabo, and Jonathan Ibrahim, who took on the mantle of leadership while continuing to serve in their operational roles.

The Nigerian military had a significant succession in the management of the national airline, Nigeria Airways, as it became deeply intertwined with both military and political influences. Figures like Group Captain Bernard Banfa, Air Vice Marshal Anthony Okpere, and another Group Captain—whose name has since faded from memory—played prominent roles during this era. But it was Air Vice Marshal Bello (rtd.) who stepped into the spotlight when he was appointed Chairman of the Presidential

Task Force (PTF) for the rehabilitation of Nigeria Airways. This task force was composed of political heavyweights, with one of its most notable members being Captain Mohammed Joji, the owner of Sky Power Express Airline. Their task was to revive the airline after a tumultuous period under two Sole Administrators, Andrew Agom and Brigadier Bajowa. These administrators had been appointed after the airline's directors were dismissed for raising ticket prices without obtaining proper approval from the Minister of Aviation.

Following Agom's regime and the tenure of the PTF, Captain Joji took over as managing director of Nigeria Airways. His tenure was marked by tension, particularly after he dismissed several trade union members, whom he suspected of opposing his appointment due to his ownership of a competing airline. Politics, as Citizen John Usein remarked on TVC's Journalist Hangout, was more than just a dirty game in Nigeria; it was a battle of survival. This political dynamic saw Andrew Agom's return to power through the influence of political heavyweights, and one of his first acts as managing director was to reinstate the union members that Joji had dismissed, with full payment of their salaries and benefits.

Amidst these power shifts, the Nigerian Army also had its moment of influence in the airline's management. A retired Brigadier-General was appointed as Sole Administrator of the airline, replacing another Sole Administrator, a decision that nearly sparked a revolt within the Nigerian Air Force. Many officers, particularly from the middle ranks, felt betrayed by their superiors, who had allowed a non-Air Force officer to take control of what they viewed as an extension of their institution. However, the military's discontent seemed to be assuaged when Air Vice Marshal Bello was named Chairman of the Presidential Task Force, with Brigadier-General Bajowa (rtd.) remaining as managing director and a key member of the task force. Eventually, Captain Joji, originally a member of the task force, rose to supersede it when he was appointed as the airline's managing director. This era in Nigeria Airways' history was a vivid blend of military hierarchy, political manoeuvring, and the constant tug-of-war for control over one of the nation's most prized assets.

During the 70th birthday celebration of Olu Bajowa, former Nigerian President Olusegun Obasanjo recounted a pivotal moment in the country's history. In his speech, Obasanjo revealed that General Bajowa had saved his life during the infamous 1976 coup d'état orchestrated by the Dimka group. This revelation stirred widespread rumours and speculation about the reasons behind Bajowa's subsequent appointment to various significant positions. Yet, this book, in its present chapter, will refrain from commenting on the administrative performance of any appointee or delving into the specifics of their management of the national airline. Such discussions often touch the realm of politics in our homeland, where appointments frequently carry undertones of political favouritism or tribal affiliations.

In Nigeria, political appointments have rarely been divorced from these influences. It is a reality that each of us sees national issues from different perspectives, often shaped by our backgrounds. However, what truly matters is merit, national interest, and infrastructural development—objectives that seem to be continually overshadowed. While there may be a need to critically examine the tenures of certain officeholders and their contribution, or lack thereof, to the downfall of Nigeria Airways, such reflections will surface in a later chapter. Over the years, many efforts have been made to transform Nigeria Airways into a more efficient, profitable entity. This pursuit of excellence even led to the airline being contracted to foreign airlines, hoping to replicate the international standards seen in other countries. Nonetheless, the national airline's trajectory has been a subject of debate, embodying the broader struggles of the nation's development efforts.

TWA: A contract was signed with the Trans World Airline of America for seven years. The contract was aimed at training Nigerian Airways employees in airline management to make the airline more efficient and profit-oriented.

KLM: The Dutch airline from Holland whose management was contracted to manage the national career for two years. During that regime, the KLM departmental directors were named as Director-in-Charge, while their Nigerian counterparts who held directorate positions were called directors. Hence in every department, we have two directors except for the personnel. In reality, the Nigerian Directors by this design became a deputy to the KLM team because the final decisions of the department are made by the expatriate teams. Anger could be seen on the faces of the Nigerian executive members team as they were surpassed in decision-making. The KLM probably suggested the idea of the Nigeria Air or they met the plan in process or they were told from the above to set it up in motion. They converted the former Nigeria Airways

Training School beside the Nigeria Airways House into a temporary head office for Nigeria Air.

The objective and plan were to split the airline into two separate organisations that will make Nigeria Airways continue to operate the domestic services while the Nigeria Air would solely be for international routes. The training school was fully furnished with the computers and equipment for the take-off on the day to be fixed in the nearest future. Unfortunately, the KLM management and contract were sacked when Nigeria's factors and tussles for power raised their ugly competitive head which led to the termination of their contract, they had to depart the country in haste and proper handover was never carried out. All the installed equipment gradually disappeared into the thin air from where they were installed. Nobody could account for the whereabouts of such capital-invented valuable items. That is Nigeria my country for you.

The KLM handed over the management of the airline to Group Captain Bernard Banfa of the Nigeria Air Force which the military government selected as managing director of the airline. The populace need not be informed of the criteria used in the selection or the experience of their choice as a platform for their selection. Nobody was sure what the mandates he was asked to accomplish except to reduce the size of the staff to the minimum manageable level through sackings, compulsory retirements and annual end-of-the-year retrenchments. Most of the previous management appointees have nothing concrete or tangible to show the world as evidence of annual reports of their achievements and contributions to the Minister of Aviation. It was an annual ritual.

CHAPTER NINE

BOARD OF DIRECTORS

IN ITS PRIME, a company of the size and sophistication of Nigeria Airways, with its extensive international network, would have required robust structures to operate efficiently and comply with global regulations. Such an institution relied heavily on its Board of Directors to ensure smooth coordination between the executive directors, the management team, and its various operations. The Board not only shaped the airline's public reputation but also served as a critical link between the organisation and the government, ensuring that the interests of all stakeholders were upheld.

Any patriot with the nation's interests at heart would expect the government to appoint individuals of exceptional managerial skill and professional repute to such important positions. In a country like Nigeria, where the constitution guarantees freedom of speech and access to information, though often underutilised, journalists should play a pivotal role in scrutinising public officials. Those appointed to serve the public must open their lives to examination, allowing the people to assess their suitability for the task.

Historically, many individuals served on multiple Boards, either appointed by military regimes or elected governments. Regardless of the process, the Boards were often filled with highly qualified professionals. Yet, despite the presence of reputable figures—senior accountants from the Central Bank of Nigeria, seasoned lawyers, and aviation experts—their efforts were ultimately undermined by greed and personal ambition, contributing to the failure of Nigeria Airways and many other national institutions. The calibre of the professionals on these Boards should have led to monumental success, but their collective failure reflected deeper systemic issues within the governance structure.

To our astonishment, the very first action taken by the newly sworn-in officials of the senior chambers of the 10th Assembly was the acquisition of brand-new cars for each member. It echoed a familiar scene we had witnessed before. Their justification? They simply could not bring themselves to use vehicles that had previously been driven by others. This attitude extended beyond mere entitlement; one of these officials, upon closer investigation, turned out to be a board member on no fewer than six different Boards of Directors. Each organisation, without fail, provided him with a new car. It led many to wonder: how many cars could a single person drive at once?

Meanwhile, their drivers, during their stops at the Motor Transport depot for fuel or a break, would often share their grievances about their employers' demands. Some of these complaints painted a picture of individuals whose actions seemed more fitting of "animals in human skin," as one might say. These privileged few embodied the biblical sentiment, "From the poor, we shall take to the rich." Their vehicles, though meant for airline duties, were frequently used for personal errands. The drivers did not complain, as they were rewarded with inflated overtime payments, all signed off by their powerful employers. No one, not even the head of audit, dared question the actions of a board member. There was one director whose driver would journey to Owo to fetch him for trips to Lagos, only to return him late on Friday or Saturday nights. Such excess made many wonder: how often did these boards meet to deliberate on airline matters?

The board of directors, a mix of professionals and politicians, were not meant to serve full-time. Yet, when they did meet, one of their first acts was to secure travel tickets for their families, often for trips abroad. This privilege was so abused that staff tasked with securing visas for official assignments found themselves arranging visas for the directors' families as well. To add insult to injury, these relatives were often upgraded to first-class passengers, despite no valid reason for such treatment. This behaviour, unfortunately, highlighted a familiar "Nigerian factor"—how power and privilege were exploited by those entrusted with public service.

The story of Nigeria Airways' board during this period is one of missed opportunities and political patronage overshadowing real progress. Collectively, most board members struggled to point to any tangible achievements or significant impact they had made on the airline. Among the few notable, yet misguided, attempts were one board member's ambitious plan to change the cabin crew uniforms from the sharp, iconic green and white British-style dress to traditional Aso-Oke, a local fabric. Millions of Naira were spent on this initiative, with large quantities of materials purchased, yet the project lacked proper testing or public input on whether the uniforms were even suitable for the airline's needs. Inevitably, the plan was abandoned, and the new uniforms never saw the light of day. No official explanation was provided about the wasted resources, nor was it ever revealed what happened to the huge stock of unused materials. They were never accounted for in the central purchasing stores, leaving a cloud of secrecy over the entire debacle.

When the board convened for its inaugural meeting, members immediately divided themselves into committees, each tasked with overseeing different aspects of the airline or investigating specific issues. Yet these committees often operated with ulterior motives. Members competed fiercely to secure international trips, whether for contract negotiations or debt settlements. The true incentive behind these assignments lies in the extra allowances and perks associated with travelling abroad on official duties. In one instance, the airline sent one of its Airbus planes to Toulouse, Italy, for major servicing as part of a contractual agreement. However, the costs incurred were far higher than what other airlines from different countries would typically pay for the same service. Corruption was rife, and contractors frequently added extra charges to cater to those who arranged the contracts. On this occasion, committee members responsible for the servicing had already provided their overseas bank account details for the contractor's "thank you" payments. But when another director caught wind of the arrangement, he flew to Italy to demand his cut of the kickback, which was promptly transferred to his foreign account.

Politically, the composition of the board reflected the spoils system that plagued many government institutions. Many appointees had failed in their political bids for Senate or House of Representatives seats, having been rejected by their constituencies. Despite their local unpopularity, their allegiance to the ruling party allowed them to land lucrative positions on the board of Nigeria Airways. One such man, deeply unpopular in his community and a member of an obscure political party, lost his local election but managed to secure a board appointment. His reward for loyalty, despite his failure at the polls, was a coveted position overseeing one of the country's most important public corporations. This narrative of political compensation over merit contributed to the airline's ultimate decline, with decisions often driven by personal gain rather than the airline's best interests.

CHAPTER TEN

HOW MD/DIRECTORS WERE APPOINTED AND REMOVED

WHEN I FIRST heard the phrase "wonders never cease," it struck me as both curious and meaningless, especially during my early years when my understanding of the world was limited by my simple, local experiences. Life, at that time, seemed predictable and straightforward. As I journeyed through different stages of life, however, I began to witness the deeper forces at play, much like trying to see through the surface of a flowing river. I came to realise that water, despite its softness, possesses the power to move pebbles and stones in its path. The old saying that "water, without hands or feet, can carry gravel along its way" started to resonate with me. This truth seemed to mirror how leaders in large corporations, like managing directors, CEOs, and executive directors, rise to their positions. While the structure may seem simple, there is an invisible current, often filled with unseen forces, pulling these individuals along to their roles.

In the airline industry, particularly in Nigeria Airways, this unseen current of power was always present, yet the process of selecting top leadership seemed puzzling. Typically, one would expect that a position of such responsibility would go to seasoned professionals—captains with decades of experience, or aeronautical engineers with practical expertise, not just academic credentials. These people were in abundance within Nigeria Airways, yet many were overlooked. Instead, the top jobs often went to those who lobbied fiercely, willing to sacrifice anything for the position, regardless of their competence. This situation extended even to the efforts of trade unions, who tried to contribute to the airline's growth through thoughtful proposals. For instance, the union once suggested improving the catering services so that foreign and private airlines could procure their food and beverages locally, which would have been a great boost to the airline's revenue. However, this proposal, filled with potential, was never even considered by the Board of Directors. It likely ended up discarded and ignored like so many good ideas that never saw the light of day. This, too, is part of the invisible force that shapes the path of progress and leadership.

Captain Tahal stood out as an exceptional leader in the history of the airline, embodying a rare blend of skill and authority. In many modern enterprises, professionals often ascend to the role of Managing Director or CEO either through strategic appointments or by rising through the ranks. Traditionally, these opportunities tend to favour the heads of key departments like Accounts, Marketing, or Planning, those who possess an in-depth understanding of a company's technical workings. These individuals, with their experience coordinating various departments, are well-positioned to drive profitability and growth.

However, in the case of the airline, merit seemed to play a limited role in leadership appointments. Historical records suggest that no Managing Director or CEO has ever been appointed purely based on qualifications. Instead, these appointments were clouded by politics and lobbying. It was not about one's track record but rather who one knew and how well-connected they were in the corridors of power. I recall stories shared by the drivers of senior directors, who were often tasked with running private errands for their bosses—errands unrelated to airline duties. It was a curious time, and I would often advise the drivers to have their bosses tune into the 4 p.m. Nigerian Broadcasting Corporation news. This news broadcast had become, in a sense, the early Facebook or Twitter, announcing appointments, removals, and sackings of airline managing directors before the official papers were even served. It was a surreal period in Nigeria's political landscape, where wonders, as they say, never ceased.

The tenure of managing directors varied greatly, dictated more by the political climate than by performance. Before 1980, an airline's success or failure was measured not by profitability or expansion but by how effectively its CEO could reduce debt. After 1980, however, domestic and international debts skyrocketed. Our aircraft became notorious, detained at airports across Africa and Europe due to unpaid handling charges, fuel bills, and parking fees. The once-proud elephant logo on our planes became a symbol of insolvency. One particularly tragic incident occurred when one of our aircraft, running low on fuel, was denied landing at multiple airports for refuelling because of our reputation for non-payment. Passed from one airport to another, the plane ultimately crashed in

Dubai. Fortunately, it was a cargo flight carrying only animals, but the loss of the crew on board was a grim reminder of the airline's deteriorating status. The aircraft had been chartered to transport livestock—goats and sheep—across countries in the Arab world, yet the identity of the person or company responsible for the charter remains a mystery to this day. The airline's reputation, once a source of national pride, had become something unspeakable, marked by both tragedy and political manoeuvring.

Throughout history, the national airline has never witnessed a woman ascend to the role of managing director, a reality that starkly contradicts the constitutional promise of equality between men and women before the law. This disparity highlights a troubling irony: despite the remarkable achievements of women across various industries, they have been unjustly denied the opportunity to showcase their capabilities within the national airline. Women have demonstrated their prowess in international diplomacy and banking, boasting impressive track records and management styles that, while sometimes unpredictable, have consistently yielded success.

One of the most notable figures in the history of Nigeria Airways was Mr. F.M.C. Obi. His tenure as managing director was remarkable not only for his leadership but also for the unique duality of his roles—he served simultaneously as the Permanent Secretary at the Federal Ministry of Aviation and as the managing director and chief executive officer of Nigeria Airways. The reasons behind his ability to hold such influential positions simultaneously may extend beyond the scope of this narrative. Here, we seek to illuminate the events surrounding the national carrier, both commendable and questionable. Readers are encouraged to form their interpretations, which may resonate socially yet be deemed technically flawed. In this nation, where freedom of expression is enshrined in the constitution, one might echo the sentiments of a lawyer in court after presenting a compelling case: "My Lord, I rest my case."

During Obi's tenure as chairman, he became a pivotal figure in the management deliberations of Nigeria Airways. Known for his hands-on approach, he delivered management proposals and projected plans to the Minister of Aviation for approval. Regardless of whether the outcomes were favourable or unfavourable, he accepted the results with an unwavering composure. One of his most significant achievements, which etched his name into the annals of the airline's history, was the acquisition of land adjacent to the Nigeria Airways House. This land became the site of new office buildings for personnel and what was fondly referred to as the "White House," the nerve centre for flight operations administration. In recognition of his contributions, the compound was dubbed "Obi Village" and remained a lasting tribute until the airline's eventual liquidation. The fate of the buildings within that compound, however, is a story for another time. It was a classic illustration of the adage that says, "Power corrupts, and absolute power corrupts absolutely."

Although operating within a democratic framework, Obi's leadership often resembled a one-man show, teetering on the edge of dictatorship. This dynamic brought with it both advantages and disadvantages; after all, it is impossible to please everyone without stepping on some toes or rubbing salt in old wounds. Those who benefited from his decisions—whether through approved contracts or appointments—hailed him as a visionary leader.

Conversely, those adversely affected by his approvals labelled him as intolerably arrogant and overly powerful. Yet, one thing remained clear: Obi's legacy was solidified by the creation of Obi Village during his time in office, a name that symbolised his status and influence. The compound was strategically positioned, sharing boundaries with the Nigerian Airports Authority Headquarters on one side and the Federal Civil Aviation Authority at the back. Inside, the buildings featured wooden fabrications housing various departmental branches, while the White House stood as the headquarters, encompassing the Operations Department, Marketing Department, and Communications Divisions.

In 2010, I found myself back at Obi Village, a place that had once been a significant part of my life. It had been 15 years since I voluntarily retired from the airline, and the changes I encountered almost overwhelmed me. As I stepped onto the compound, I was struck by the sight that greeted me. What was once a bustling hub of activity had been transformed into a series of cubicles, repurposed by money changers known as Bureau de Change. The nostalgia hit hard, and as I made my way to the office I had once occupied, I felt my emotions welling up. Tears streamed down my face without my realizing it until the Mallam attending to me in his cubicle noticed my distress. Concern was etched on his face, and he asked if I was experiencing eye pain, pointing out that my eyes were wet and tears were dripping down my cheeks. In a moment of self-comfort, I quickly composed myself, attributing my watery eyes to the dust blown in from outside, reluctant to reveal the deeper shock of witnessing the state of my former workplace.

The contrast between my memories and the present was stark, echoing the broader struggles within the airline industry. Each year, the Managing Director was tasked with submitting a detailed report to the Minister of Aviation, outlining both achievements and the challenges faced in meeting operational targets. These reports revealed a grim reality: the airline struggled with mounting debts, staff retrenchments, and accidents that had plagued its operations. The focus had shifted dramatically since 1983 when chief executives were primarily judged on how many staff members they could cut. The goal of enhancing the airline's growth through academic qualifications and relevant work experience seemed to take a back seat. Instead, the age-old tradition of nepotism and connections dictated employment opportunities. During my time in personnel, I had the rare privilege of sifting through the files of staff—both open and confidential—giving me a firsthand view of how deeply ingrained these practices were in the hiring process. It was a bittersweet realisation, watching how the principles of meritocracy faded away in favour of who one knew in the industry, leaving behind a landscape far removed from the vibrant airline I once knew.

In the corridors of our workplace, certain staff members were regarded as "untouchables" or "Ostriches," a designation stemming from the peculiar privileges they enjoyed, such as overseas duty tours that consistently favoured them over their senior colleagues or those directly accountable for specific assignments. It was a perplexing system, where merit often took a backseat to favouritism. Those bestowed with such opportunities accumulated foreign currency, and with it, a sense of arrogance that made them look down upon their peers. This growing discomfort among department heads led to occasional retrenchments, as they sought to distance themselves from this privileged class. In the world of Nigeria Airways, power dynamics were ever-changing; one's job security felt like a fleeting mirage, susceptible to the whims of those with influence.

Among the ranks of our colleagues was a man from another department, a frequent companion at the Sky Power Club. His career trajectory was remarkable, marked by annual promotions and a steady stream of overseas assignments that filled his pockets with foreign currency, be it dollars or British pounds. My curiosity piqued, and I felt compelled to uncover the source of his rapid ascent. The revelation came as no surprise: nestled within his employment application was a business card bearing the name of a former President of Nigeria, a token of introduction that proclaimed him to be a protégé of the managing director at the time. This revelation only deepened my understanding of the underlying currents of power at play.

During Captain Tahal's tenure, Alhaji M.T. Bature served as Personnel Director before his promotion to Managing Director. He was supported by Captain Nnachi, a figure often described as "no-nonsense." Together, they formed a formidable team, committed to revitalizing the airline. Despite their best efforts to turn things around, they found themselves thwarted by a lack of governmental support, a stark reminder of how the aspirations of individuals can be stifled by the broader institutional framework. In this complex tapestry of ambition and politics, it became evident that no position was truly indispensable, and the delicate balance of power could shift in an instant.

HOW MD/DIRECTORS WERE APPOINTED AND REMOVED

The Nigerian Air Force (NAF) gradually fostered a desire for ongoing control over the national airline, a move rooted in its military establishment. This ambition was ignited by the controversial appointment of a retired Army Officer as the managing director of the airline—a decision that sparked outrage among middle-class officers, who perceived it as a blatant violation of their domain. The tensions were palpable; it felt like rubbing salt into an old wound. Before this Army Officer took the helm, Group Captain Banfa had served as managing director, his reign marked by terror and authoritarianism. A man driven by his sense of power, Banfa surrounded himself with aides and guards, prowling the airport grounds at night. He would target night shift workers, meting out brutal punishments for minor infractions, often taking delight in showcasing the military's dominance over "bloody civilians." Innocent employees, some of whom had dedicated decades to the airline, were subjected to merciless beatings and arbitrary detention, a cruel reminder of the military's heavy hand.

Amidst the chaos of Banfa's leadership, two contrasting narratives unfolded. One involved a seemingly inconspicuous staff member working in revenue accounts—an unassuming cashier handling cargo clearance payment. This man, with his appearance reminiscent of a devout Jehovah's Witness, donned the most inexpensive clothing, often arriving in tattered shirts and dilapidated sandals purchased for mere naira at the Ikeja roundabout. However, beneath this façade of piety lay a web of deceit. An investigation, instigated not by the company's Audit Division but by an external entity, uncovered a staggering betrayal. This so-called innocent account officer had drained the company's resources, leaving it on the brink of destitution. To the shock of his colleagues, it was revealed that he owned two large hotels and operated a fleet of six trucks distributing beer and soft drinks. Three of these trucks were eventually seized and displayed at the airline's headquarters for all to witness. Initially, the officer vanished into obscurity, but when his wife was arrested and taken into military custody, he resurfaced, forced to confront the repercussions of his actions. The outcome of this scandal remains shrouded in mystery, with the case file inexplicably lost and the vehicles ultimately returned to him, suggesting that in the murky waters of corruption and money laundering, negotiations often take precedence over justice in modern Nigeria.

In the turbulent history of Nigeria's airline industry, no one could claim to be a saint, whether military or civilian. During the tenure of Banfa, the airline faced a significant tragedy when one of its F-28 aircraft crashed, resulting in a total loss. Despite this incident, the remaining F-28 planes, which boasted exceptional equipment and facilities for landing and take-off under any weather conditions, were abruptly sold off to unknown contractors without any due process. Shockingly, one of these aircraft ended up as the presidential jet for the late Libyan leader, Muammar Gadhafi. This prompted a flurry of questions about the rationale behind selling two perfectly functional aircraft and the lack of accountability for such a decision. Banfa faced no inquiry or requirement to explain his actions before being reposted back to the Nigerian Air Force, leaving many to ponder the integrity of the management process.

As has often been the case, most appointed Managing Directors (MDs) seemed to measure their performance solely by the number of employees they had retrenched or retired each year. Retrenchment, which meant removing an employee before they qualified for retirement, contrasted sharply with retirement, which occurred upon reaching the statutory age or after serving the airline for a designated period. The concept of "redundancy" rarely made its way into the administrative goals of the airline. Following the retrenchment and retirement announcements of December 1986, several affected individuals challenged their dismissals in court, arguing that they had not been provided with reasons for their termination. In response, the airline quickly crafted a new template for retrenchment letters, including vague justifications that were deemed unchallengeable in Nigerian courts. One notable instance involved the sudden retirement of a director, justified by the assertion that he could no longer "cope with modern technology" in aviation. This was a bitter pill for many long-serving employees who had dedicated decades to the airline, often serving in high-ranking positions and possessing advanced qualifications. Among them was Mr. Sam Epelle, who spent over ten years as the airline's representative in Europe, having climbed through the ranks over thirty-three years of service. Such dismissals were dishonourable, especially when contrasted with the elaborate parades typically associated with military retirements.

Despite a directive claiming the workforce was too large for the number of aircraft operated, the reality was starkly different. Retrenched employees faced a future without reemployment in the same organisation, and the principle of reducing the workforce was often disregarded. Just three months after any retrenchment, a flood of applications for new hires would arrive, courtesy of politicians, military elites, and business magnates. The management often found themselves pressured to consider these applications, violating the very regulations they were supposed to uphold. One striking case involved a woman in Human Resources who was retrenched but later reinstated due to external pressure, illustrating the uneven application of rules. In this environment, it became clear: not all fingers are equal.

CHAPTER ELEVEN

THE ROLES OF AIR TICKET AGENTS

IN THE EARLY days of commercial aviation, airlines individually chose the people or companies that would represent their interests in selling flight tickets to travellers. There were no overarching guidelines or regulations from international bodies to ensure standardisation or uniformity across the industry. Instead, the relationship between the airlines and ticket agents was established through direct contracts. Once these agreements were in place, the agents would act on behalf of the airlines, selling tickets to consumers in exchange for immediate payment, whether from the traveller themselves or a third party paying on their behalf, though notably, payouts from other agents or travel businesses were excluded.

Ticketing officers, who might either be direct employees of the airline or independent agents working under contract, played a pivotal role in helping passengers arrange their trips. Their duties extended beyond mere ticket sales; they answered questions about routes, schedules, and travel arrangements, confirmed reservations, calculated travel expenses, and facilitated the sale of tickets. These officers were the face of customer service for airlines, ensuring that travellers' needs were met with friendly and efficient service. From handling reservations and check-ins to addressing travellers' concerns and finding solutions to meet customer needs, airline ticket agents were integral to ensuring passenger satisfaction. Their responsibilities encompassed a wide range of services designed to streamline the travel experience and maintain the airline's reputation for service excellence. They are,

1. Excellent customer skills
2. Good communication and interpersonal skills
3. Able to work under pressure
4. Good numeracy and literacy skill
5. Knowledge of relevant computer system
6. Bank guarantor that remittance of tickets sold is paid to the airline.

In accordance with the requirements outlined in the preceding sections, it becomes evident that managing an air passenger travel ticket agency was a costly and intricate endeavour. The nature of these businesses demanded regular inspections and audits to ensure that financial returns accurately mirrored the number of tickets sold. Agents, often contracting with multiple airlines, strategically diversified their customer base across different carriers, ensuring flexibility and wider reach.

The physical outlets of such agencies were expected to reflect the spirit and identity of the airlines they represented, or the destinations they catered to. This was often achieved through carefully curated décor, featuring photographs and images that highlighted the airline's fleet or the tourist attractions of the countries they served. The selection process for these agents was fiercely competitive. Only those with a proven track record of strong sales, accountability, and financial reliability were shortlisted for interviews. These candidates needed to demonstrate that they could handle large volumes of sales while ensuring timely payments for the tickets sold. For those aspiring to become agents of Nigeria Airways, specific criteria had to be met. One of the key factors was the size and location of the business, which had to be strategically positioned to attract and impress customers. Moreover, the agent needed to have the financial capacity to purchase and sell a substantial number of tickets, ensuring the airline had sufficient passengers to maintain its flight operations.

Historical records indicated that summer was consistently a peak travel season, with Africans journeying to Europe and, in turn, Europeans and Americans flocking to Africa. Similarly, during the Christmas season, many travellers from Europe and America ventured to Africa, allowing airlines to capitalise on this surge by raising airfares. These peak periods provided a vital cushion to the airlines by helping them mitigate the effects of lower passenger numbers during the quieter months, especially when schools were in session. In a dramatic turn of events, several ticket agents took Nigeria Airways to court in Europe, accusing the airline of breaching the terms of their contracts. This legal battle unfolded amidst the backdrop of political turbulence in Nigeria. With each change in government, particularly when one civilian administration gave way to another from a different political party, ripples were felt across various sectors of governance.

The new political powers, eager to reward their loyalists, often sought to restructure existing agreements, displacing former allies to make room for their own. In the case of Nigeria Airways, this led to the abrupt termination of commercial contracts. It was not just the politicians at play, those in the airline's management also sought to secure their influence and power. Eager to expand their reach, they replaced long-standing contracts before their tenure expired, further fueling instability within the airline's operations.

In Europe, however, these actions came at a significant cost. Nigeria Airways found itself facing the scrutiny of the judicial systems in both the United Kingdom and the United States. The airline was heavily fined for failing to adhere to the strict legal frameworks governing contracts in these countries. The courts were unyielding, holding Nigeria Airways accountable for its disregard of international law and contract regulations, marking a significant chapter in the airline's tumultuous history.

When an opportunity emerged for a contract to be reviewed such as an air ticket agency, those staff in related positions to make detailed analyses would be bombarded by pressure with complementary cards and notes of assistance of who is who in politics, military, traditional, rulers, and top government officials. Where one fails to play the game to meet their demand or expectation, one will become either an immediate target to get rid of, or when the time of retrenchment comes often in December every year, the period supposed to be for joy, happiness, promotion, award of wages increase and bonuses you can be sure that the number one on the list of people to be purged from your department or division could be you. Because the exercise was often conducted in top secrecy and confidentiality, one would not have a wind of what was coming, the paper would just arrive on your table. Therefore, some people who are politically or socially connected get their businesses registered as ticket agents without having to go through the requisite procedures. These groups of people are the ones whose books were never balanced and staff efforts to enforce the regulations such as suspending their licence are often frustrated by instructions from the above to lay off their hands from the procedures of auditing, I have tried to make some personal investigations why some glaring cases were abandoned by the airline before they became public or newspapers sensations. The people concerned or involved are not questionable because they realise, they belong to the class they termed "the untouchables" in society.

International ticket agencies in Europe and America often become rigorously and fiercely competitive mainly because of the people who want to use them for one reason or the other. These agents are usually of various nationalities and they are prepared to use all ammunitions in their warehouse to wage the commercial war. Desperation has some senators moved which has no healthy business motive but personal ego and personal gains. There was one clear issue which could be the basic platform for this ruthless war, experience showed that Nigeria businesses in Europe and America were prone to breaches of rules and regulations through shortcut syndromes and once this occurred, courts of law often imposed severity of fines on any litigation breach of contract.

There are many Nigerians in the United Kingdom and in the United States of America who have all the criteria required to be a ticket agent for the national airline but because those who are indirect beneficiaries do not want their identities to be exposed, they prefer to deal through foreigners, especially if they were feminine. Women cannot be forced to divulge information. In a turn of events rooted in privilege and power, a Lebanese woman was granted the exclusive right to sell Nigeria Airways tickets in the UK. Confident in the strength of her connections, she believed that the contract was hers for as long as she wished. However, when a new government came into power in Nigeria, the privilege was swiftly transferred to another agent. Faced with this unexpected loss, the woman sought justice in court, her last recourse in a fight she had not anticipated.

Her struggle echoed another high-stakes situation from Nigeria's past, for example, the mysterious case of the £2.8 billion petroleum revenue. Allegedly deposited in a UK bank, the vast sum of money was moved from bank to bank, each transfer designed to maximise the interest it accrued. The money became untraceable as it was shuffled under different names, lost in a complex web of transfers that few could remember, let alone unravel. Those involved, all people of privilege, carefully orchestrated these movements, benefiting from the growing interest abroad.

For years, the whereabouts of the money remained a mystery, until one day, a Nigerian newsreader broke the silence with a shocking revelation. She announced on live television that the money had been traced and located in a bank account. The aftermath of this revelation, however, took a darker turn. The identity of the account holder was never made public, and instead of being hailed for her courage, the newsreader was unceremoniously fired from her job. Her dismissal was swift and final, a poignant reminder of the saying, "When two elephants fight, it is the grass that suffers." In both stories, privilege shielded the powerful, while those who sought justice or truth found themselves vulnerable, their voices silenced, their efforts thwarted.

When a contract with a U.S. agency was abruptly terminated, a determined woman took legal action against Nigeria Airways, citing a breach of contract. Rather than appoint a qualified legal representative, one of the airline's executive directors, unfamiliar with U.S. court procedures and lacking the necessary evidence to counter the woman's claims, chose to represent the airline. Predictably, the court upheld the prosecutor's case. Nigeria Airways was heavily fined and ordered to pay substantial compensation for the breach.

This legal loss came when the national airline was in financial struggles, particularly in Europe and America, despite robust ticket sales through agents in those regions. The situation had become so dire that the airline's manager resorted to using his salary and allowances to pay the local staff's wages. British law, notoriously strict about employers failing to meet wage obligations, left the manager with no choice.

The same legal principles applied when the airline eventually went into liquidation. In line with local redundancy laws, all staff employed in the UK and the USA were paid their due entitlements. Some workers in the UK received thousands of pounds in compensation. However, the situation was tragically different for the airline's employees in Nigeria. There, workers were left to suffer in silence, enduring poverty, deteriorating health, and family separations. Children were unable to attend school, families were evicted from their homes as breadwinners could no longer afford rent, and many were forced to return to their ancestral villages, broken and disillusioned by the airline's collapse.

CHAPTER TWELVE

CONTRACTS AWARD

IN CONTRACT LAW, two fundamental elements must exist: an offer and its subsequent acceptance. Typically, the offer comes from the party requesting goods or services (the offeree), who may make this request verbally or through advertisements. The party making the offer (the offeror) responds by providing a detailed proposal, including design specifications or descriptions of the goods, alongside a price list. After a period of negotiation, once both sides reach an agreement, the contract becomes legally binding upon acceptance of the terms.

This straightforward procedure, often observed in theory or academia, can unravel in complex real-world scenarios. A case in point is the plight of a national airline, bound by contracts it neither initiated nor requested. Many of these contracts were thrust upon the airline, and orchestrated by powerful individuals in positions of authority. Often, these contracts emerged not from legitimate business needs but from the personal ambitions of political insiders with a stake in the outcome.

It was not uncommon for political elites to exploit their connections within the airline to further their financial interests. They would often rely on insiders, employees within the airline, to uncover potential avenues for personal gain. For instance, in the property division of the airline, a staff member might suggest the idea of constructing a new building at one of the country's airport stations, such as Kano or Port Harcourt. This suggestion could then be followed by a commissioned architectural design, complete with a list of required materials and estimated labour costs.

However, such projects were typically initiated without prior consultation with airline management to assess whether the construction was necessary or beneficial. These proposals, bypassing due process, often found their way to the President or the Minister of Aviation, accompanied by a complimentary card from a well-connected individual of influence. Ignorant of the actual needs or implications for the airline, the President or Minister might approve the project, forwarding it to the airline's managing director for consideration and action.

In turn, the managing director would send the proposal to the appropriate department head for analysis, seeking advice on how best to accommodate this high-level request. And so, the wheels of unnecessary, sometimes crippling, projects were set in motion, projects that saddled the airline with perpetual debt, born not out of operational necessity, but out of political manoeuvring and personal gain.

In the course of its operations, the airline found itself burdened with numerous houses rented and furnished under procedures that became a significant financial drain. Yet, a far more crippling blow was the decision to hand over the airline's management to KLM. No sane management team would propose such a reckless and chaotic plan to the government for adoption. Despite KLM and the airline both serving as passenger and cargo carriers, their operational environments were fundamentally incompatible.

This topic warrants a deeper dive, and I will explore it further in a later chapter. At this point, it is important to understand that whenever the director sought to return with recommendations to the Managing Director, the process was a mere formality. The director would often consult experts such as the company architect, quantity surveyor, or finance officers. However, in reality, no director had the courage or authority to defy what had been mandated by the President's office at Aso Rock. The director's tenure was entirely dependent on staying in the good graces of the President.

What typically occurred was that once a project proposal was submitted, the individual behind it would work tirelessly to ensure its approval, often relying on personal influence, whether through persuasion, bribery, or intimidation. The method depended on the reception they encountered. The closer one's connections to the presidency, the greater the mobilisation fees one could extract from a contract. Unfortunately, many contracts remained incomplete or abandoned, even though hefty mobilisation payments had already been made. Such incidents were common across almost all departments within the airline.

Even the Board of Directors was not immune to these practices, frequently accruing unnecessary debts for the airline. This was especially true for the female board members, who wielded significant political influence, either through party affiliations or direct connections to the seat of power. There was one notable instance when the airline was tasked with reroofing the home of a board member in Ikoyi. Not only was the roof replaced, but new doors were installed to her liking, and granite was spread along the footpath, all at the airline's expense. How such an irrelevant renovation for a private residence, neither owned nor rented by the airline, received approval defied all principles of accountability.

Some executive directors breached their contract of employment by not protecting the commercial interests of the airline by abusing their official positions. For instance, there was a period when the airline was not flying any aircraft either lack of serviceable aircraft even for domestic operations. But for reasons best known to some caucus of top few management teams for a weekly ₦1m. IOU, i.e., cash in the form of a loan was regularly released to catering services and within two days the IOU would be replaced with vouchers for purchased items which was not delivered and not used. This was going on for months and the audit's attention was hinted about it but no positive action was taken to block the leakage. The syndicate was traced to four influential directors and controllers who were responsible for the processing of disciplinary action against staff. One of the side effects of the syndicate action was reflected in management's decision to rehire the Head of Audit back to the service of the airline on contract after he has retired on completion of the mandatory 35 years when his previous services in other organisations were merged with the services of the airline. He was retired on grade level 16 but was rehired on grade level 15. Within one year of his rehire, he was promoted back to grade level 16. The Union's bone of contention against this type of action was that there were younger people in the division who had the same or greater educational qualifications and had served the airline for years which qualified them for an upgrade to the position of head of the audit but their star was not allowed to shine and their quality of performance was always depressed. The Union agitation was once again ignored.

CHAPTER THIRTEEN

STAFF CONCESSIONAL TRAVEL TICKETS

IN THE LATE years of Nigeria Airways, public discontent often arose from two primary sources: personal grievances and broader corporate failures. The personal criticisms were not directed at specific individuals like Mr. A or Mrs. B, but at the unfortunate staff who became the face of the airline's inefficiencies. When a flight was delayed or, worse, cancelled, it was the staff, station managers and airport workers, who faced the passengers' wrath. The abuse they endured was harsh and public, even though the causes of such delays were frequently beyond their control. Yet, the frustration of waiting passengers was understandable. They were impatient, often unaware that the delay, far from being a mere inconvenience, might have been a stroke of fate, preventing a tragic accident and saving lives. In our frustration, we often fail to recognise this other side of the coin.

As a wise man once said, "We cannot all sleep with our heads facing the same direction." If we all thought the same, viewed life through identical lenses, and acted in the same way, the world would lose its richness. There would be no diversity of thought, no intellectual challenges, and no room for ambition or competition. Imagine, if you will, if all Nigerians practised the same religion, held the same profession, or engaged in the same trade. Where would be the variety on our dining tables, the different styles of fashion in our wardrobes, or the unique furniture in our homes? Even in Russia, a state that once projected itself as the epitome of communism, where equality was supposedly the cornerstone of society, the collapse of that system revealed deep disparities. The films that emerged after the fall of communism showed that some lived far better lives than others under the same ideological banner.

Meanwhile, back in Nigeria, rumours swirled around certain government institutions, like the Central Bank, of employees enjoying generous salaries and enviable benefits. Some reports even claimed that certain staff members were paid not in local currency, but in the coveted American dollar. It may well have been idle gossip, a way of tarnishing the reputation of the institution—but, as the old saying goes, "Where there's smoke, there's fire." People's lifestyles often betray the truth behind the rumours, and Nigerians, with their keen eyes and ears, are not so easily deceived.

The same scrutiny fell upon the nation's petroleum refineries. Year after year, funds were allocated for maintenance in the national budget, yet the refineries remained dormant. What benefits have these refineries brought to the people when they have been out of service for so long? The questions linger, as do the frustrations of a populace that demands more than just empty promises and inaction.

One of the key reasons Nigeria Airways staff faced public resentment was the special travel privileges they enjoyed, both domestically and internationally. These benefits were not granted by the airline's management or the Ministry of Aviation but by the International Air Travel Association (IATA). This global policy applies to all airline employees across the world. According to IATA's regulations, staff travel is a standard benefit for airline workers, as well as others in the air travel industry. This includes their family members or close friends, often referred to as "buddy passers." Staff could purchase tickets at a significantly reduced rate, but only if there were unsold seats available on the flight. These discounted tickets were a common practice throughout the aviation sector.

In Nigeria, however, the public widely misunderstood these benefits. Many believed that Nigeria Airways staff could simply grab tickets at will and fly anywhere in the world, as though the airline were some sort of benevolent gift-giver. I even recall a few friends telling me that I could travel whenever and wherever I wanted. Of course, there was no truth in this; such perceptions were entirely exaggerated and unfair. Nigeria Airways employees were no different from their counterparts at British Airways, Lufthansa, Air France, Virgin Atlantic, or any other airline. The travel privileges they enjoyed were identical to those granted to airline workers worldwide under IATA guidelines.

According to these rules, staff could access concessional tickets only under specific conditions. The employee had to be on annual leave, and the ticket was only valid for the duration of that leave. Additionally, the cost of the ticket was minimal, typically covering just the printing costs in the country where the airline operated. Family members also had access to these discounted tickets, but only if there were available seats on the flight.

It is important to differentiate between these personal travel privileges and official trips. When airline staff were sent on official duties, whether within Nigeria or abroad, it was a different arrangement entirely. This was no unique perk for Nigeria Airways staff, companies across various sectors in Nigeria, including the Nigerian Ports Authority, the National Electric Power Authority, and the Nigerian National Petroleum Corporation, all covered their employees' travel expenses when they were sent abroad for work-related purposes. These trips were for training, seminars, equipment inspections, or negotiations, and the companies provided round-trip tickets and an estacode to cover living expenses during their employees' absence.

Thus, the travel benefits that Nigeria Airways employees received were no different from those enjoyed by their peers in the global aviation industry. Misunderstanding this led to a great deal of misplaced criticism and resentment towards them.

There is empirical evidence that PHCN workers enjoy some special discounts over the settlement of their electricity meter readings in their houses, which is another form of conceptional. The staff of the Central Bank could easily purchase their foreign currency without hassles when travelling abroad. It was generally assumed that the workers at the NNPC have some privileges exclusively provided for them when they want to buy petrol for their cars. Probably they have a special ticket that gives them some percentage discount at petrol stations. It was generally assumed that the travel ticket concession enjoyed by the staff of the airline was a policy introduced by the management of the airline. Bearing in mind that Nigeria Airways was a member of the civil aviation cartel worldwide, it is bound by the rules and regulations set in place by the international body that supervises and governs civil aviation as an organisation. It down how many tickets a staff could obtain in one year and how the ticket costs should be determined in local currency which varied in value when compared with the dollars or sterling used as a yardstick. Also, the cost of printing the ticket locally is different from one member country to another. To achieve uniformity, it was approved in their code of regulations worldwide that airline should charge their staff the cost of printing the ticket in their countries. Therefore, it can be seen that Nigeria Airways management only endorses the mandate given to them. After all, the management and their family members were bound to enjoy the same privilege.

The number of tickets to be approved which should go through so many processes of checking documents of the individual including the application form which must be accompanied by an annual holiday approved paper in one year is prerogative to approve what is suitable for their economic interest and what their trade union could negotiate. In Nigeria Airways, the management approved a maximum of four tickets for domestic travel and the period of the travelling was administratively restricted and pegged to the period of staff annual leaves, although the door of usage was opened to allow the ticket to be used at weekends which does not interfere with the official working days of the week of the staffs. For international travel facilities or conditions, the staff could

STAFF CONCESSIONAL TRAVEL TICKETS

obtain two tickets per person and use them during their annual leave. It is important to mention that some workers in sensitive positions and routines could not avoid proceeding on full annual leave at one time, therefore, the staff annual leave would often be split into times that are convenient for them, hence granting tickets to meet the need of the workers when granted the annual holidays. Don't call me the 'Mr Nigeria factor', if we want to be honest with ourselves, there is no sense in either denying its existence or minimising the gravity of its effect on either individual on all organisations or government policies. Everybody is free to make their assumptions on the impacts either positive or negative the Nigerian factor had marred or promoted the image of Nigeria as a country.

Whatever the preventive measures any organisation may set in motion to ungalvanized fraud in our community, it could be seen and later noted that it would be circumvented. This confirms the common saying that the white man who invented the pencil also invented the eraser to clean the unwanted words. Therefore, if you give human beings, like Nigerians, an inch of space of freedom, they will attempt to give themselves an extra ten more spaces. That is what makes human beings less satisfied and always asking for more like Oliver Twist. There is no way I will ever state that staff of the Nigeria Airways were saints, wherever laws and regulations you adopted to avoid smartness, they would make sure they beat you to your own game. Some staff travelled over and above their privilege illegally as they connived with people entrusted to make the issue of the ticket. In every society, there must be a black sheep. The airline section administers the sales and issuing of tickets to the staff on official duty tours and those proceeding on annual holidays or their families. Because of the poor supervision by the managers that headed the section, reports were emitting that corruption and atrocities were rampart at large scale for a very long time.

There was always the issue of fast guys who would like to have more than their fair shares of anything out of greed and they were often prepared to have their desire at any cost, including bribing their ways. As it is with the governors, so it is with the members of the House of Assemblies, you find them in the board of directors, in executive directors, how do you want the ordinary people to control themselves in similar circumstances? As we used to say in Yoruba, "The flying birds in the sky may not know or be aware that the people on the ground are watching its movement". Had the number of new tickets released for issue been properly checked with the number issued, checking with the names reconciled, and serial numbers, the fraud could have been nipped in the bud and greater surveillance put in place to avoid repetition. Many people were able to obtain far more tickets than the number approved for them and their families without due process. By the time the alarm bell was raised, many people were put on investigation and suspension and the list of people was compiled.

There are many staff, especially, the ladies who are on the list of people that were culpable in the ticket manipulations. They became overnight travellers who bought and sold clothes, clothing materials and gold for their private business shops and to be sold to other staff during working hours. They travelled out on Friday night to London, did their transactions at Liverpool

STAFF CONCESSIONAL TRAVEL TICKETS

Street, Dalston and Shoreditch areas on Saturday and Sunday and departed London on Sunday night, and they are in Lagos on Monday morning. Anybody can come to work late on Monday morning, you can give excuses for some traffic congestion or children's care. What a brisk business and cool additional income to augur the family income.

The administrative process of handling such reported cases was never followed and all corrections pointing out what the disciplinary procedures should be were deliberately thrown overboard. It came to light that some senior officers in charge of the implementation of the disciplinary cases were indirectly involved as they introduced people from outside the airline to the staff to help with staff tickets, hence to avoid the cat spilling the beans, those involved were just suspended and later summarily retired with full entitlements. The audit division had failed in its duties by not detecting the abnormalities and discrepancies in the number of issued tickets, the names on the approved official forms and the amount remedied to the cash office. You can call me a speculator.

Fingers are never equal; hence, people pursue different interests to prove that ego. There are some staff, particularly the women, who are more professional traders in terms of buying and selling than other staff of the airline who sit down on a chair and look at the books. As earlier stated in this chapter, some women pursue their private interests parallel to the terms of their employment. Those who are observant could see them hassling up and down the corridors of the buildings of the airline. Though to some extent it might not affect their efficient performance and their punctuality to duty. The latter must suffer on the way of the other either because they were somebody's wife or mother to some children.

There has never been any doubt in me that I should have faith in God and I need to call on Him regularly in my medium of prayers. As my close friends always call me, "Man of little faith", in my heart and connection to my maker, they were wrong. Simply because I did not frown my face when fasting, attended church every day of the week from Monday to Sunday or obeyed my pastor's commandment whenever he asked members of the congregation to assemble in the church for one reason or another does not make me an unfaithful or unreligious person. Whenever I got to work, the first thing I always did most committedly was to pray in silence. The prayer may take different dimensions depending on my environment and the challenges I intend to confront that day such as the people, (co-workers or visitors) determining my mode of prayer and preparedness. I could sit down on my chair and silently pray, the length of the prayer on what problem may arise during the day counts. I do not worship my God like the Pharisees who want to be seen on roadsides or shouting to be praying.

Some people cause trouble for themselves intentionally or unintentionally, and the problem could be foreseen and avoidable or divertible. People always assume that the devil or Satan moves about in the air or resides in their houses and can visit anybody at any time it desires. My philosophy of life is completely different from these analogies, devil or Satan whatever you prefer to call him, if in existence, has its abode where it hibernates in the body of a human, but human being often knocks on their doors and forces themselves to make an entry into their territory. On the one

STAFF CONCESSIONAL TRAVEL TICKETS

hand, trouble does not look for people, on the other hand, it is the people who look for trouble. That was why they said, "Don't trouble troubles, except trouble troubles you." Somebody who works under me went to the house of the devil one day and I was nearly dragged inside the abomination where the devil dwells.

By the virtue of my job description, one of my assignments in the last eight years in the airline was to travel from one station to another station to issue identity cards for new staff or renew the expired or about-to-expire ones, since the company identity card (ID) be that of staff or their family members have an expiring date on them. Arrangements were made for me and the airline photographer to undertake the tour of most stations once a year at different times. The standard arrangement was for the photographer to burn or destroy the expired ID cards and take a photograph of staff to produce another ID, once that was done, we would return to base in Ikeja. Unfortunately, on a few occasions, some cards were hidden which made them reusable for any sinister motive some other days or some other years later still bearing my signature.

There was one particular day when nothing seemed to be in order, then I looked round and I could not pinpoint what the issue was that might have caused the anxiety. Later on, in the afternoon, a security staff I recognised and knew well but was attached to the properties division of the airline came to the office to collect his family identity cards which had been issued awaiting collection. Initially, I did not notice that he was watching me intensely but his actions and attitudes were glaringly noted by some of the staff in the room. He was not in the mood for "yabis" as he used to do with the secretary and other staff whenever he came to the office or when we met at the social club for our usual socialisation. But as he was about to exit from the office my sectary asked me in a low voice and signal to look up and see the person who was looking at me intensely, as he got to the entrance door our eyes cut each other, he looked back at me with curiosity and that made my secretary ask me to look up at the man going out. As I lifted my head and asked him if he had any queries on what he had collected before I could alter a word, he was the first to remark and that remark was astonishing. He said to me ironically, "Baba Jooo" which was one of the many nicknames some people gave to me, "Your body is smelling" in Yoruba. I was astonished and tried to persuade him to come back to the office to enlighten me on what he meant, but he jammed the door and left. I even ran out to call him and ask him for an explanation for what he had just said, but with my naked eyes, he picked up a race and disappeared.

With that unsolicited remark, I could sense that there was a big problem looming like a tsunami on me or my employment or my section. I became confused and all my staff were also down casted as we had never heard of nor experienced such a situation in our years of working as a team. But a bad event happened on a day probably unprepared for, and they said nothing can fall from the sky that the land cannot accommodate. On enquiry, I got to know that a day before at the Murtala Muhammed International Airport, a person presented himself with a staff ticket and identity card to travel to Jeddah in Saudi Arabia, but because his face was not familiar to the counter checkers, they asked him what department he worked in the airline and he told the staff that he worked the personnel department and the staff identity card in his possession says the holder works in Engineering and Maintenance department at Kano Station. Overnight, His identity card and travel ticket were seized but allow to go back to his house. An official report on the incident was compiled and sent to the MD office. It was said that my signature which the informant told me was a long bridge as people described it, that was on the ID card

The Station Manager's report was minute to the Director of Human Resources who is supposed to handle such incidental reports but because it involved me who was never in the good book of the director and wanted to show himself as not connected; he minutes it to one of his subordinates called controllers to issue me with a letter of sack. There was a possibility of erratic action by the director which may side-track the laid down procedures of query, explanations in terms of reply from me and probably the setup of a committee to deliberate on the matter. The Controller took the letter to him to remind him of the procedures that are entailed on a matter of that nature but as he disagreed and insisted on what must be done in his way, the Controller told him to handle the matter himself and drop the letter on his table. This was as a result of personal advice I gave him when he was posted to the new department which did not go well with him.

Let me remind the readers that the director was promoted to that post from another division which could not be disputed but some of the surroundings of the appointment had grey areas. He was from the same ethnicity as the then managing director which all the staff termed as, crony. It further revealed that after the MD had retrenched over 36000 workforce in December 1986, as the reorganisation of the airline. Ironically, two controllers in the Personnel were on the same level with the new appointee and they have been on that level for over five years. To make his position robust and lucrative, he transferred the purchasing division and the properties division and merged them with his new position.

Probably, he was trying to seek people's opinions about his appointment and the re-organisation that had just been set up and implemented. In one of the conversations at the time he resumed duty, I congratulated him and expressed how fortunate he was that purchasing and property divisions could be put under the Personnel department. I told him as a Yoruba man to another Yoruba man that he needs to be careful as any abuse of power is always draconically dealt with. I gave him instances of his predecessors who were summarily removed from their posts unceremoniously. Instead of him appreciating and following my wisdom of words, he took offence and was looking for vendetta and was asking his syndicates to listen to what I told him.

By virtue of this airport incident, I was not expecting fairness in the disciplinary procedures should the matter related to me be referred to them for deliberation. Later, I learnt that my suspicion was correct when the paper of the fake traveller got to his table, maybe he did not want to be accused of witch-hunting or deliberate victimisation, he called an enlarged number of people for deliberation, about twenty in number. The matter was already tabled and discussed and some people were already interrogated as I was made the last person to be called without pre-warning in a letter form or verbally invited to the committee meeting.

While the matter was still in a stalemate, people who were aware of what happened started to write letters protesting to exonerate themselves from the incident. A messenger in the department claimed that the fake man gave him ₦20,000 to facilitate the issuing of the ID, and the staff ticket, stating how he distributed the cash, how much he gave to the photographer, and how much he gave to one in the staff ticket office. whom he gave money and how much he gave to them. He confirmed that I knew nothing about it in the presence of the committee members. The idea of querying was that it happened under my nose.

When the committee set up to investigate the case finally called me on the matter was merely to hear how the staff identity card, which we used for someone about four years ago was still available for another person. How many such cards were illegally and fraudulently used for people without my knowledge could only better be imagined than envisaged.

ONE WITH GOD IS
PROTECTED AND SAFE.

CHAPTER FOURTEEN

V.I.P CONCESSIONAL TICKETS

IN THE UNIQUE nation of Nigeria, an intriguing dynamic exists within the halls of power and influence. It is the only country known where the wealthiest and most influential individuals, when not on diplomatic missions, enjoy the luxury of travelling nearly free on their national airline. They pay only a fraction of the ticket cost compared to the average passenger. This advantage is not merely a reflection of financial privilege but stems from a deeply rooted network of connections, woven through shared school experiences, ethnicity, marriages, and elite social clubs. Every successful figure in Nigeria, whether they acknowledge it or not, is linked to someone in a position of authority.

This web of relationships defines much of Nigeria's societal fabric. In a land where ambition often surpasses qualifications or experience, individuals reach heights that may seem unattainable or unimaginable to outsiders. It is a culture that thrives on bold aspirations, even when such dreams appear far removed from one's formal education or practical expertise.

Like families, nations are intricate networks of people bound together by shared interests and circumstances. Nigeria, composed of many families, communities, and histories, reflects this truth. However, its unique structure often leads to situations that other nations might find perplexing.

In contrast, other nations like Saudi Arabia have shown remarkable feats of personal commitment to national causes. I once read in an international publication that the King of Saudi Arabia purchased fifteen 747 aircraft for his country's national airline out of his pocket. This gesture was not a mere show of wealth but a reflection of deep national interest.

Yet, in Nigeria, the lines between wealth, power, and public accountability are often blurred. The nation's history is marked by lingering mysteries, such as the unresolved disappearance of $2.8 billion in petroleum funds, funds that, to this day, remain unaccounted for. Stories of such magnitude are not found in local newspapers, where editors have faced tragic fates, including assassination in their own homes. Decades have passed, and investigations still hover in limbo, leaving a void in the pursuit of justice.

Meanwhile, the free press has thrived in countries like the United Kingdom. Two morning papers, the "Metro" and "AM", once stacked in train stations and public spaces, offered the public easy access to information at no cost. These newspapers, funded by private enterprises, were a testament to the value placed on sharing knowledge and privilege.

It is a reminder that, when blessed with abundance, be it wealth, influence, or privilege, one must share it with others. This is the true measure of leadership and responsibility, and it is a principle that resonates beyond national borders.

There was once a unique newspaper service, freely available for the public to pick up on their way home after work, designed to keep people informed of the day's events. Imagine, if a similar initiative were to be introduced in Nigeria, groundnut and puff-puff sellers would likely take advantage of the free publication, collecting as many copies as possible for their personal use. Even local thugs might seize the opportunity, positioning themselves as self-appointed agents of these vendors to make a daily profit.

In another sphere, the list of individuals granted reduced concessional tickets to fly first class on international journeys remains elusive. If such a list were ever published, particularly in certain Arab nations, it could spark a public uproar. Many of the individuals on this list could easily afford private jets or even contribute an aircraft to their national airlines out of a sense of nationalism. But this concept of nationalism, where does it truly exist in people's attitudes? Too often, it seems like a word paraded only by ministers and directors of NGOs to showcase their so-called service to the public. In truth, as the old saying goes, "the evils that men do live after them; the good is often buried with their bones." This could not be more fitting for Andrew Agom, a man whose life and legacy must be shared, though sadly, my readers will never meet him, for he has tragically passed away. May his soul rest in peace, and may his family find the strength to bear this irreplaceable loss.

Andrew Agom was a man of many perspectives, seen differently by different people, depending on their relationship with him. An American-trained engineer, Agom carried himself with the confidence of someone who believed that every problem had a solution. His approach to matters was direct, often dismantling challenges as if they posed no difficulty at all. This mindset likely developed during his time in the United States, shaping his behaviour and beliefs.

At a crucial moment in Nigeria's aviation history, the management of Nigeria Airways decided to raise passenger ticket prices without prior approval from the Federal Ministry of Civil Aviation. This unilateral move led to the dismissal of all the airline's executive directors, except for Andrew Agom. Instead of being fired, he was appointed Sole Administrator of the airline. It is often said that politics is a dirty game, and indeed, one can meet the same people on the way down as on the way up. In Nigeria, climbing the ladder is rarely about merit alone. There is always someone behind the scenes pushing a name or a résumé into the spotlight. But staying in a high position is another story entirely. As the wise say, you can be helped to get a job, but no one can help you keep it.

To remain in a high-ranking role, especially in a national airline, is a precarious task. Every decision and posture is scrutinised, either praised or condemned, depending on the interest groups involved. In Nigeria, a nation full of many ethnicities, each group tends to favour their own in filling lucrative government positions. This competition can lead to one's downfall if not carefully navigated.

Agom's rise in Nigeria Airways was unexpected. Years earlier, he had applied for a Grade Level 09 engineering job at the airline but was deemed unsuitable and his file closed. This happened before

General Obasanjo handed over power to the civilian administration of Alhaji Shehu Shagari in 1979. When the new government came into power, a new Minister of Civil Aviation, hailing from the same state as Agom, reviewed his failed interview and appointed him to a much higher position: Principal Purchasing Officer on Grade Level 12, bypassing Level 10 and 11 entirely. By the time Agom resumed his duties, the colleagues who had passed the original interview remained stuck at Level 09.

Before Agom's appointment, each department at Nigeria Airways fiercely protected its interests, including procurement, though payments were processed centrally by the finance department. Agom, however, quickly changed that. Within a year, he gained the authority to centralize purchasing for all departments, marking his arrival as a new and powerful force within the airline.

At that time, I was the Administrative Officer of Motor Transport, and our work was linked to his. Agom was responsible for ordering fuel and signing off on deliveries, ensuring that everything matched before payment was authorized. His meticulous attention to detail and control over processes quickly made it clear that a new king had indeed ascended to the throne.

To avoid being seen as interfering in others' affairs or stepping into areas outside my jurisdiction, I developed a habit whenever the fuel truck arrived at our site. It usually came in the evening, after office hours. I would send a driver to his quarters in the Government Reserved Area (GRA), tasking him to handle the delivery himself. This way, he could, personally, compare what was delivered with what he had ordered. Yet, each time he arrived, he was always furious, reminding me that he had verbally instructed me to sign on his behalf. His reason was simple, he knew I worked late every day.

The tanker drivers, known for being sharp and dubious, often made it necessary to measure the fuel delivered into the underground tanks, ensuring it matched the quantity ordered. Any discrepancy had to be accounted for by measuring what remained in the tank before delivery. This responsibility, entrusted to me by Agom, showed the trust he placed in others. His free-spirited nature allowed him to delegate such a critical task, demonstrating not only his trust but also his willingness to share responsibility.

Nigeria Airways was an amusing yet treacherous place, where good intentions could easily be misinterpreted. People were often blamed for being overzealous or nosy, and it was essential to tread carefully to avoid being wrongly accused.

Then, there was that extraordinary incident. After serving the company for just one year, Andrew was promoted to Grade Level 13, an Assistant Manager position. The promotion letter was handed to him by a messenger, and as the process required his signature, the messenger waited for him to authenticate the delivery. However, Andrew, in his usual meticulous manner, insisted on reading the letter before signing it. The messenger, with little choice, allowed him to do so.

Upon reading the contents, Andrew erupted in a fit of anger, speaking in American slang that few could understand. He felt it was an insult to be promoted to Grade Level 13. His protest escalated, he tore the letter in half and threw it back at the messenger, flatly refusing the promotion. The humiliated messenger returned to the personnel department, unsure of what to do next.

Remarkably, the situation took an unexpected turn. A new letter was issued, promoting Andrew to Grade Level 14 instead. How this happened remains a mystery. Meanwhile, those employed before him were promoted only to Grade Level 10.

In just two more years, Agom was promoted, yet again, this time to Controller, a Grade Level 15 position equivalent to Deputy Director. His rapid ascent created tensions among his colleagues, many of whom felt unfairly treated. However, any attempts to protest promotions were perilous. Employees who dared to file petitions often found themselves facing retrenchment or early retirement. It was said that the investigations into such complaints were superficial at best, and the act of raising grievances often became the grounds for termination.

When Mr. Zakaria Haruna, the Director of Engineering, retired, Agom was appointed to succeed him, even though several controllers were senior to him for many years. I will not speculate or call names, as it is best to let sleeping dogs lie.

Just a few months into his role as Director, a new scandal erupted. The Federal Ministry of Civil Aviation accused the airline's management of raising ticket prices without proper approval or consultation. For this breach of procedure, the entire management team was swiftly retired en masse. Yet, once again, Agom was spared from the purge. No explanation was given for his exemption.

As the highest-ranking officer left standing, Agom was appointed Sole Administrator of the airline, a position created just for him. It was an unprecedented move, and he wasted no time implementing his vision. He reorganised the management team, putting his favoured candidates in key positions, and reshaped the Managing Director's office to project the image he wanted.

However, Agom's rise was short-lived. His candle, burning from both ends, eventually flickered out. Without any formal explanation, he was dismissed from his position. In the eyes of the Presidency and the Ministry, no reason was ever needed to justify the removal of their appointees. Legal challenges were futile. While former workers and members of the public occasionally took the airline to court, cases related to retrenchment or retirement were often endlessly adjourned, designed to wear out any legal opposition.

Agom's journey through the ranks of Nigeria Airways was as swift as it was dramatic, leaving behind a legacy that sparked both admiration and resentment.

Once upon a time in aviation, an operational manager for a domestic airline found himself at the centre of an intense drama. On what seemed like an ordinary day, he had dispatched a flight bound for one of the northern airports. The plane had already taxied out of its parking spot and was queued on the runway, ready for takeoff, when he received an urgent call from a senior military officer. This officer, once a member of the cabinet, demanded that the manager recall the flight. His reason? The officer's lady companion was running late and still on her way to the airport.

With respect and professionalism, the manager apologised and explained that the flight had already been dispatched. The schedule could not be altered. But the military man was adamant, commanding the manager to call the plane back to wait for the lady. Once again, the manager apologised, explaining that he lacked the authority to reverse the flight's course. Not only would recalling the aircraft violate international aviation regulations, but it would also infuriate the passengers already aboard. He assured the officer that the lady could be accommodated on the next available flight.

Furious, the military man slammed the phone down. The manager assumed that was the end of it, but he was gravely mistaken. The officer had more power than he imagined. Within hours, the military man called the airline's managing director, accusing the manager of insubordination, twisting the conversation to paint a picture of rudeness and defiance. Without so much as a formal inquiry or a chance to defend himself, the manager received a letter of compulsory retirement. It was a cold dismissal, blaming him for inefficiency despite over a decade of loyal and exemplary service.

Devastated and demoralised, the manager sought to clear his name. He reached out to his direct supervisor, the director of operations, hoping for support. But his pleas fell on deaf ears. When the managing director refused to grant him an audience, he had no choice but to seek justice through the courts. He hired a reputable lawyer and took his case to trial.

Yet, the proceedings were a farce. The airline, notorious for such cases, never sent a defence counsel to contest the suit. For years, the case dragged on, whistling into oblivion, like so many others before it. The airline, safeguarded by top-tier law firms like the chambers of Rotimi Williams and Ikomi, paid hefty retainers to defend against their own employees' claims, ensuring that cases quietly disappeared without resolution.

This incident was not an anomaly. It was one in a series of legal disputes between staff, contractors, and the now-defunct Nigeria

Airways. The airline's operations were marred by mismanagement and legal manoeuvring that often shielded it from accountability.

One can look back further to the downfall of another key figure in the airline's history—Agom. As he rose to prominence and solidified his position, it seemed he was on the verge of transforming the airline into a profitable, expanding entity. But suddenly, without warning, he was dismissed. His sacking, announced during the four o'clock news, shocked the staff, dashing their hopes that he could be the one to lead the airline to new heights. It was a harsh reminder of how even the mighty could fall, like dry leaves in the chill of winter.

After Agom's departure, Captain Mohammed Joji of Sky Power, a former member of the Presidential Task Force (PTF) under Air Marshal Bello (retired), was appointed as managing director. The airline, already fragile, entered a period of further instability. Divided interests plagued its leadership, and the company, already a mere shadow of its former self, barely held together. Much of the turmoil during Joji's tenure was later exposed during an inquiry into the airline's mismanagement. But, like so many inquiries before it, the findings were buried, never acknowledged by the government, nor were any actions taken. It became another wasted exercise in futility, a cover-up, lost to time and neglect.

During his time in office, many aspects of Joji's leadership raised eyebrows. One of the most glaring controversies involved allegations that Joji personally pocketed millions of dollars in cheques meant for Nigeria Airways. These cheques, purportedly issued by the Presidency and the Ministry of Aviation, never seemed to reach the airline's accounts. However, the accusations remained elusive, more rumours than solid fact, as no evidence ever surfaced to back up the claims.

Yet, if these allegations had been true, several questions would have demanded answers.

- First, whose name appeared on the cheques?
- If they were issued in Joji's name, who processed them, and for what official payments were they issued?
- If the cheques bore the name of Nigeria Airways, how could a bank allow them to be deposited into a different account, possibly Joji's? Surely, the bank staff should have recognized the difference between Nigeria Airways and any other entity, including Sky Power Airline, or even Joji himself.

Such a scenario seemed implausible, though, in Nigeria, stranger things had been known to happen. Recently, a newspaper story detailed a similar incident, where cheques and documents meant for one person were manipulated for another's benefit. The story involved two childhood friends. One, Mr. A, pursued higher education in Mass Communications, while the other, Mr. B, could not afford university and started working, saving diligently for a car.

Years later, when Mr. B had saved enough to buy a second-hand car, he turned to his old friend, Mr. A, for assistance. The pair travelled from Ibadan to Lagos to find a vehicle, eventually settling on a Mitsubishi for ₦650,000. Unknown to Mr. B, Mr. A had secretly struck a deal with the dealer for a ₦10,000 commission. After purchasing the car, Mr. A drove them back, but just outside Ogere, he attacked and killed his friend, hiding the body in the bush. Mr. A then registered the car in his name and drove it for a year before the police solved the mystery. This tragic tale illustrated just how easily trust could be betrayed and, disturbingly, how money and documents could be fraudulently altered.

If such deceit could occur on a personal level, what could be expected from those in positions of power? Joji, during his tenure, promoted a woman from grade level 09 to 14 without the usual procedures, raising murmurs among staff, but with no formal channel to challenge such favouritism. In addition to alienating his employees, Joji was accused of systematically silencing union leaders by either retiring or retrenching those critical of his leadership.

After years in the political wilderness, Agom, another key figure, returned to power. Having learned hard lessons during his period of unemployment, Agom carefully played the political game to regain his position as managing director of the airline, ousting Joji in the process. This time, Agom was more cautious, aware that not everyone who smiled in his face wished him well. He also recognised the immense power of the federal government, which could destroy a person through design or accident.

One of the most egregious scandals involved the airline's concessionary tickets, issued to Nigeria's elite. While the public believed these figures could afford their first-class travel, many were flying on heavily discounted or even free tickets, granted by the managing director's office. To keep this operation hidden from regular employees, a special office was established under the managing director's supervision. Anyone with a connection to the government could request these benefits, often bypassing the president altogether. Requests were processed quickly and quietly, with bribery becoming the norm to expedite matters.

As the abuse of these privileges escalated, family members and even housemaids of the well-to-do benefitted from free tickets. The scope of this corruption became clear during an investigation into the airline's mismanagement. Two secretaries were found responsible for financial irregularities, one was ordered to repay ₦6 million, the other ₦4 million. Yet, the inquiry never reached the heart of the matter, how tickets were funnelled from Aso Rock to the privileged. That arena remained untouchable, shielded from scrutiny.

By the time Nigeria Airways resorted to hiring planes and crews to serve to pay passengers, it was clear the airline was carrying too much weight in the form of nearly free first-class travellers. This drain on resources, coupled with widespread mismanagement, crippled the company's ability to turn a profit and meet its obligations. It was, in many ways, the ultimate "Nigeria factor", a perfect storm of favouritism, corruption, and inefficiency that spelt disaster for the nation's once-promising airline.

CHAPTER FIFTEEN

PURCHASE OF AIRCRAFT FOR THE AIRLINE

AN AIRCRAFT OR plane, whichever category you put it, is suitable for conveying passengers from one place to the other by air. In our analysis, the aircraft must have been manufactured by a reputable company licenced by the IATA to produce commercial uses—passengers and cargo which separate it from private jets which were for the owners, their family members and friends. Like other commodities, aircraft manufacturers give extensive advertisement for their products because of the heavy capital investment, it appeals to a specific type of people, corporate bodies or government agencies interested in their product with features that make it special and appealing to be added to their existing fleets of planes.

The most important aspect of advertising the sale of aircraft is to show specialities which they have just developed in such areas as engines, interior design facilities or passengers' capacities and assurance that it will last and durable for many years in terms of durability. It is the responsibility of the buying company to evaluate the suitability of the mentioned features that it will suit the purpose of their purchase. Any individual or corporate body that has a purpose for any aircraft and has purchasing power could request a brochure and may order one.

The method or procedure of purchase is a little bit more advanced than that of the purchase of a car either by cash in terms of a debit card or on higher purchase terms which involve monthly payment which will embody the addition of interest rate. Insurance of an aircraft is complicated and requires some specialised procedures. We must realise that the manufacturers have acceptable Insurance companies in their country of manufacture or countries of purchase in case of disputes or putting up claims. Most of the aircraft in the fleet of Nigeria Airways accident of curiosity which was only the characteristic of a country like Nigeria. Every month, brochures of existing and new aircraft were received by the company and there are shelves where they were stored and displayed in a library format. Sometimes they were in alphabetical order for easy location. This is to enable either inspection or location made easy for picking up should it be required.

Whenever the airline requests the purchase of a new fleet of aircraft such as Airbus A 310 or DC 10, such request must be formally forwarded to the Federal Ministry of Aviation which will study the proposal on the grounds of suitability, maintenance, capacity and commonness from the companies that have already taken delivery of the particular make to ensure its reliability. The airline's request, recommendation and approval of the ministry would be forwarded to the Presidency by the Minister and when he receives approval the Minister would forward it to a committee that may comprise people of different expertise such as finance, marketing, engineering, aeronautic and other fields that may have substantial contributions to be inclusive. Now that we are in a democratic dispensation, the Senate and the House of Representatives have a committee on how we are daily breathing not in terms of medical facilities but scrutinising whatever is related to the function as it must have their stamp of approval before it can become law. There is an existing committee on Aviation from both chambers that monitors what the minister is doing and how the ministry is performing its duties. There is always cause for complaint of delay as virtually every committee takes time before they look into matters referred to them. They often claim that they work on a first-come, first-served philosophy.

The procedures in Nigeria Airways cases are laid down and written in very clear language as follows:

Step 1: The Director of Operation, a flight Captain in that 2nd rank must receive the brochure for the sales of a new product. i.e. a commercial or cargo aircraft.

Step 2: The Director will form a committee of knowledgeable people and specialists in aircraft. They will deliberate, and if the aircraft is found suitable to join the fleet of the company, the maintenance and Engineering will be co-ordinated to express their opinions on how the aircraft can be serviced within their available equipment and facilities.

Step 3: The reports with the brochure would be sent to the managing director for consideration and to be tendered at the board of directors' meeting for further studies, reports and further considerations.

Step 4: The Board, if satisfied with the request, will send it to the Legal Department which will scrutinise the bolts and joints of the legal implications and recommend a proper approach including the areas concerning insurance and inspections.

Step 5: The company will select an aircraft broker. Their job is to assist a company in buying or selling an aircraft. Their job is similar to a real estate agent as they present all information on the aircraft in the market. Nigeria Airways which has been in the business of aviation for some time must have had a reputable broker where purchases of aircraft are brought into the matter.

Step 6: A Letter of Intention (LOI) is drafted in the general terms of purchase which would be set for the purchase price, amount to be deposited, arrangement for pre-buying inspection and the expiration time for the offer.

Step 7: The buyer may select an external agent for comprehensive inspection by a facility familiar with the type of aircraft the purchaser is buying, this is a critical step in the purchasing process. The maintenance facility produces a list of discrepancies they discover during their inspection.

Step 8: The aircraft will be delivered to the buyer once the deposit has been made and other details have been ironed out. The chairman of the Board of Directors with the Managing Director is always at the Presidential tarmac at the domestic wing of the

PURCHASE OF AIRCRAFT FOR THE AIRLINE

airport Ikeja for the official handover with some dignitaries to witness the special handover of the aircraft.

Most of the analyses I have made above were just protocol procedures or a channel that requests for the purchase of an aircraft passes through in theory. The story is an entirely different one when it comes to practicality. There was never a request to purchase an aircraft from Nigeria Airways to the seat of government that ever-yielded natural results. There is always a Nigerian factor in every transaction of the airline. For a request to be read and put on an agenda for mere consideration not to mention approval, there must be somebody along the corridor of power who will broker a deal to get the matter to a higher level. There are so many men and women highly connected in the world of purchase of such items that if you ignore them your request would die a natural death from an infant. They may not necessarily go to ask for anything from the airline direct but they were expert in making their own money from the manufacturer or their agents.

Once they are informed informally by their inside agent, they will obtain special price quotations from the manufacturer or their outlet which will have no relevance to the brochure price list. Nobody is going to ask questions nor counter-check what the brochure price is compared to the quotation submitted. They were experts on how to take care that no eyes would turn around and no vetting would go into those areas. To deal with Nigeria, most foreign companies know that Nigeria is a special customer they have to play ball or a game that needs to be revealed to their home government or not to the Nigerian government. The philosophy has always been "chop and let me chop", and once you are reluctant to play the ball in their way and terms, they will take their customary to another body. You who ignored them are the one who will regret your ignoring their presence and fast lane they could have taken your matter through.

The sellers have to promise so many bodies as they visit their showrooms or factories as members of certain committees that are working for the Federal government in the interest of the airline. Let me give a typical rumoured scenario of the purchase of an aircraft for the national airline. The executive directors of the airline would form several different committees to study the brochure and look at different feasibility studies of how the particular advantages the purchase of the aircraft will bring to the airline. This could be the top echelon of the airline comprising the directors of operations as the head of the airline pilots who will fly the aircraft after it has been delivered. Next is the director of Maintenance and Engineering who will service and repair the aircraft after purchase. The Director of Finance will be paying for the aircraft in the near future. The Director of Marketing who will be responsible for the sales of the passenger tickets, and the Head of Legal matters should see that Insurance is available and other documents as contained in the terms of purchase and maintenance are in order.

The board of directors' members may likely follow in the footsteps of executive directors. The Ministry of Civil Aviation will likely be the next to go on a duty tour to inspect the progress so far made in assembling the aircraft. The Senate and House of Reps committee on aviation will be next in the queue. Each committee will leave Nigeria Airways with their estacode but expect to be lavishly accommodated and entertained by the management of the airline manufacturing firm. All attending groups were recorded as a unit. Should the purchase go through, each member of the committee will be settled in recent times, we read about the Aviation scandal where the foreign contractors contracted to expand the runways in some of the national airports were told to raise their quotations to make provision for the minister and officials Kickbacks. We have read about the Halliburton scandal, and the Ministry of Aviation inflation of contracts and currently we are hearing FIFA's allegation that Nigeria and Haiti members were trying to sell their votes to the highest bidders.

Even Lord Sugar, the popular business mogul in the United Kingdom who became, a member of the House of Lords knew that to influence British business with the world at large once made a remark about Nigerians which attracted both the reaction and receiving end of his excellency the Nigerian High Commissioner to the United Kingdom, Dr Dalhutu Saeki Tafida for insulting Nigerians for making demeaning and spurious comments on Lord Sugar BBC show apprentice owner. Lord Sugar was said to have suggested that Nigerians could not be trusted over financial promises. The argument to justify or to go about the remark depends on the land the individual built their camp. For those who want to retain neutrality, there is sufficient evidence to support Lord Sugar's statement while those who are the Apostles of rebranding Nigeria will shout crucify him. But as Jesus said to the woman accused of fornication in the Bible, the issue is who is holy to first throw the stone at the woman, but since nobody did, she was asked to go and commit no sin any more.

Reliable information available showed that before you can transact business with the state or Federal governments of Nigeria, once you have the correct contact you would be encouraged to inflate your quotations to create enough capacity for extra dollars to be distributed during or after the contract was approved to wet the pocket of those who helped you to get the required approval. The corruption in this area is so endemic and epidemic to the extent that aircraft major services which could not be undertaken at the airway hanger are flown abroad, some are done in Ethiopia or most are undertaken at the Air Lingus in Ireland which was subject to feedback to the pocket of those who are the PR to the government and some key officials whose connection influence the power to obtain the necessary approval for the contract to be executed.

From the above analysis, it can be seen that the price of the aircraft is never universal for all customers. Giving quotations of price to the Nigerian government or agency must have a reservation to accommodate all sorts of numerous expenses that will arise after sales and special interests. When Alhaji Sanusi, the onetime former Emir of Kano was appointed as the governor of the Central Bank of Nigeria, he attempted to clean the staple of the irreparable commercial banks' staples. This led to some Directors, Chief Executive Officers and Executive directors of banks being forcefully flushed out then corruptive practices enquiries were exposed. This showed that no area of the national economy is clean.

CHAPTER SIXTEEN

WORKERS UNIONS CONTRIBUTIONS

IN THE HISTORY of Nigeria Airways, the presence of multiple trade unions reflected the professional diversity of its workforce. Pilots had their union, as did engineers, while the majority of workers, those in personnel, accounts, cabin crew, and other departments, belonged to broader unions. Among the various unions within the airline, two stood out as dominant, spreading their influence across the entire civil aviation industry, from the Ministry of Aviation to other parastatals.

For many years, the Nigerian Union of Air Transport Service Employees (NUATSE) emerged as the most influential union within civil aviation. Its reach extended beyond Nigeria Airways to include entities like the Nigeria Airports Authority, the Federal Civil Aviation Authority, and even the workers of foreign and private airlines. NUATSE became the collective voice for those who felt voiceless in the industry. With membership expected from all but the most specialized professionals, joining was almost automatic upon employment. Those who preferred not to participate could opt out by signing a formal declination form. However, for most employees, signing the membership form ensured a monthly deduction from their salary, which was channelled towards union activities.

The funds collected through these deductions were used to maintain the union's secretariat and support its staff, while also financing trade union programs. Active union members were often sponsored to attend both local and international conferences, gaining exposure and insight into trade unionism on a global scale. Some were even sent to places like Russia and Czechoslovakia (before the country's political split) for training that could last up to five weeks. These opportunities enriched the members, equipping them with the knowledge to contribute more effectively to union activities back home.

Despite the benefits, rivalry often emerged, particularly during elections for key union positions at the national level. Nigeria Airways, being the largest contributor to the union's membership, held significant influence, particularly through its unified technical service employees. Behind them in membership size were the Nigeria Airports Authority and the Federal Civil Aviation Authority. While private airline workers were also union members, their numbers were much smaller.

NUATSE was led by a strong General Secretary, a formidable figure capable of challenging industry management and presenting informed counter-proposals. One such leader, Mr. Austin Momodu, became known as a fierce advocate for workers' rights. His professional trade unionism made him a formidable negotiator whom management often avoided when delicate union matters arose. He was especially known for educating companies on avoiding layoffs, recognizing the profound impact job loss had on workers' families.

Within the union, competition between the three main branches, Nigeria Airways, Nigeria Airports Authority, and the Federal Civil Aviation Authority—was constant. To prevent any one branch from dominating the union's leadership, national offices were allocated through careful negotiation and compromise. However, some branches, particularly the Nigeria Airports Authority, engaged in manipulative practices, failing to remit the full union contributions collected from their members and blocking national secretariat staff from reviewing their payrolls. When complaints arose, rather than support the union's goals, they often threatened to break away entirely.

Every four years, national conferences were held at Murtala Mohammed International Airport, marking a grand occasion where elections for union officers took place. These events were not only political but educational, with specialized officers from the National Labour Conference and Trade Union Congress giving speeches on trade unionism and discussing the future of the labour movement in Nigeria's commercial development. They also oversaw the election process, ensuring that the leadership team for the next four years was fairly chosen.

However, relations between the union and Nigeria Airways management were often tense, especially under the leadership of Managing Director Mohammed Joji. Joji, unaccustomed to the collaborative role unions played in operational decision-making, found their involvement frustrating. His reluctance to engage with the union was compounded by rumours that funds, meant to elevate the national airline, were not reaching its accounts. Union officials grew increasingly frustrated with his evasiveness, culminating in a dramatic moment when they barricaded him in his office to force a meeting. When Joji finally conceded to the meeting, he claimed ignorance of the issues raised and offered no solutions.

This era of fierce union activity within Nigeria Airways reflected the broader struggles of labour movements across industries—an ongoing negotiation for power, voice, and influence in the evolving landscape of Nigerian aviation.

Within two years of taking office, he began to target certain branch officers whom he believed were at the centre of union opposition to his leadership. Convinced that these individuals were loyal to his predecessor, Agom, and not to him, he either personally selected or instructed the personnel department to select these officers for dismissal. As a result, these workers were terminated from the company and left unemployed for nearly four years. During this time, they received minimal support, sustained only by small contributions from fellow union members.

When he was eventually ousted and Agom was reinstated as managing director, one of Agom's first actions was to reinstate the dismissed union members. He ensured that they were not only brought back into the company but also received their full back pay, including allowances, as though they had never been dismissed.

During this turbulent period, the executive officers of the airline's branch would frequently dedicate entire Saturdays to brainstorming sessions. They worked tirelessly to identify the airline's problems and develop proposals aimed at improving profitability. These proposals were carefully studied, approved by the union's general membership, and forwarded to management for consideration. However, the relationship between the union and management was fraught. Time and again, it seemed that management and the union were headed in entirely different directions, like two parallel lines that would never intersect. The union's recommendations were routinely dismissed, as management held ultimate authority over the airline's policies and had different priorities.

Matters deteriorated further after the death of Austin Momodu, a well-respected national secretary of the union. His successor, a politically motivated figure, exacerbated divisions by favouring the NAA (Nigeria Airways Authority) branch, sowing discord among different union branches. Under his leadership, the idea of forming a new Senior Staff Association began to take shape. The NUATSE (National Union of Air Transport Employees) was to remain the union for junior staff, while the newly formed Air Transport Service Senior Staff Association of Nigeria (ATSSSAN) would represent senior staff. Consultants were hired to select a name, draft a constitution, and establish the new union. Mr Aiyede, an outsider to the aviation industry, was appointed general secretary of ATSSSAN. This move angered NUATSE members, particularly at the NAA branch, where tensions nearly boiled over into violence. They saw the formation of ATSSSAN as an affront and began labelling its leaders with derogatory terms.

The transition to the new union was meant to be straightforward—anyone at or above grade level 07 would automatically become a member of ATSSSAN, while those below that level would remain with NUATSE. However, NUATSE members staunchly resisted this change. They rejected the idea that grade level should determine union membership and opposed the automatic transfer of senior staff to ATSSSAN. The airline's accounts department was instructed to deduct union dues for ATSSSAN members at grade level 07 and above, but this led to protests and demonstrations.

The conflict eventually reached the courts, with ATSSSAN seeking legal recognition of its constitutional right to represent senior staff. NUATSE, on the other hand, filed a counterclaim disputing ATSSSAN's constitutional framework. After hearing arguments from both sides, the court ruled that staff at grade level 07 and above were to be members of ATSSSAN, while those below would remain with NUATSE.

However, the court's decision proved difficult to enforce. In Nigeria, it was not uncommon for court rulings, particularly during the military regimes, to be ignored. Even though the court had spoken, the practical implementation of the ruling faced obstacles, including resistance from the Nigeria Airways management. Behind the scenes, it became clear that management was sympathetic to NUATSE, possibly out of fear of the union's militant tendencies. Peace meetings between the unions, called by the airline's Controller of Personnel, repeatedly descended into chaos, with insults and accusations flying across the table.

Ultimately, the management's reluctance to enforce the court's ruling only deepened the divisions between the unions, prolonging the conflict and leaving the airline's labour relations in disarray.

ATSSAN took proactive steps to present numerous proposals to the management of Nigeria Airways, suggesting ways to restructure the airline's catering division. Their recommendations centred on turning the catering unit into either a separate company or a subsidiary, independent from the core airline. In their detailed report, ATSSAN outlined the necessary changes for international airlines and private domestic carriers to select flight menus that included diverse international options. They also emphasized how Nigeria Airways' catering services could become globally competitive by enhancing their on-flight menus to meet international standards.

With insights from experts in the airline's engineering and maintenance departments, ATSSAN convened an ad-hoc committee meeting with the Ethiopian Airlines union. Their report showcased how Nigeria Airways could continue to carry out various classes of aircraft checks—from A to D—as Ethiopian Airlines had been authorised to do in Nigeria. The report emphasized that the manpower was readily available, and only the necessary equipment and inspections were required to convince IATA (International Air Transport Association) that Nigeria Airways was capable of performing comprehensive aircraft maintenance.

Additionally, ATSSAN proposed upgrading the airline's ground equipment used for aircraft servicing. They suggested renting out this equipment to smaller and foreign airlines, which could generate significant revenue and improve the financial standing of Nigeria Airways. They also highlighted the potential of the underutilised cargo shed; with proper management and facility upgrades, it could become a profitable venture for the airline.

Another area of focus was the Property Division, where ATSSAN proposed serious housing renovations. They suggested that it be managed as a separate company or subsidiary to streamline operations and revenue generation. The Sports Club, an airline social hub where staff gathered after work to socialize and hold events, was also mentioned. The Club had once held vast acres of land, but much of it had been forcefully taken by a Golf Club through military influence, without any compensation. ATSSAN noted that the land, situated close to the airport, was valuable enough to host a five-star hotel.

However, despite the clarity and potential of these proposals, they were shelved by successive management teams. No white paper was ever produced to indicate any discussion or serious consideration. Over time, Nigeria Airways House and the Maintenance and Engineering hangar were handed over to Arik Air, seemingly free of charge. There was no record of any payments made to the liquidated airline's account, leading to widespread speculation about the true ownership of the airline. In a turn of events, the Obi Village, once an important part of the airline, became a bustling market and hub for Bureau De Change (BDE) operations. The iconic White House at Obi Village, which once housed the Flight Operations, Marketing, and Communications divisions, was reportedly gifted to a lady by the government. The Finance Office building, which once handled the airline's cash flow and revenue, was handed over to a bank, while other structures were transformed into a marketplace for currency exchange.

One day, while visiting Obi Village, I wandered back to my old office, curious to see what had become of it. To my dismay, the office I once knew had been partitioned into six cramped cubicles, each occupied by men conducting currency exchange deals. Their agents ran about, enticing customers looking to buy or sell dollars,

British pounds, or other foreign currencies. The sight raised a question in my mind: when will we learn to build on the legacies left by our predecessors, rather than letting them crumble?

Thankfully, the catering division was spared from the same fate that befell Nigeria Airways House and the maintenance hangar. Instead, it was occupied by the union, serving as a venue for staff verification during pension payments and as a church where congregants gathered to pray. They prayed for the government to release the remaining balance of the retirees' pensions—prayers directed at those in power who seemed indifferent to their plight.

GOD IS PATIENT.

CHAPTER SEVENTEEN

CATERING SERVICES

THE CATERING DIVISION of Nigeria Airways held a strategic location, nestled between the domestic and international wings of Lagos airport, right after the Nigerian Air Force Lagos headquarters. It was an odd and somewhat puzzling placement, hidden from the main road connecting both airports and situated far from the Nigeria Airways House and Obi Village, where many operational branches were based. How the airline acquired such an obscure site remained a mystery, but what was indisputable was the division's crucial role in the daily operations of the airline.

The Catering Division's impact on the airline's success cannot be overstated. In the competitive world of air travel, airlines often build their reputations not just on punctuality and pilot expertise but also on the quality of customer service, which extends to the in-flight experience, including meals and beverages. Nigeria Airways was known for its timely take-offs, though, as often happens in aviation, flight schedules were primarily controlled by the Federal Civil Aviation Authority (FCAA), which determined domestic flight rosters. Even as passengers rushed to board their flights, and private airline agents worked tirelessly to check tickets and ensure valid travellers passed the gates, Nigeria Airways staff remained composed, watching the controlled chaos unfold. Reports surfaced of touts exploiting this rush as early as 5 a.m. at the Lagos local airport, reflecting the bustling nature of air travel at the time.

The eventual fate of the catering building tells a story of transformation. After Nigeria Airways was liquidated in 2003, the space became the headquarters for the airline's trade union. It also served as a place for Friday prayers, where former employees gathered, hoping for divine intervention to resolve the ongoing struggle for their unpaid pensions.

Although President Buhari approved a sum of ₦78 billion to settle the debts in 2018, only half of that money reached the former staff, the rest shrouded in secrecy. Rumours swirled that the Accountant General might have invested the remaining funds in lavish estates and malls, leaving the former workers in financial limbo, begging for justice and the means to live a dignified life.

Staffing the Catering Division mirrored the recruitment processes of other departments within the airline. The Head of Catering would submit a request for new hires to the Managing Director, justifying the need for additional staff. If approved, the request would pass to the Director of Human Resources, who would oversee the recruitment process. Advertisements were posted, qualifications outlined, and interviews conducted, though, as was common in those days, external influences often played a role in determining the final hire. Once hired, the pay grade for new employees was already determined by the original request, cementing the structured hierarchy of the division.

Running the catering department was no small feat. It involved purchasing vast quantities of food and materials, similar to household shopping but on an industrial scale. The quality of the meals served on international flights had to meet the standards of global airlines, requiring the catering staff to undergo regular training and briefings. In Nigerian culture, the head of such a division was often expected to be a woman, and during Mrs Aladejana's tenure, there were few complaints from travellers. However, when a man replaced her after her voluntary (or possibly forced) retirement, he struggled to maintain the same level of service. His downfall came when security discovered catering items in the trunk of his car, leading to his dismissal. Thus ended his brief stint as head of a division that had long played a vital role in the success of Nigeria Airways.

At that time, Group Captain Banfa was the administrator of the airline, and he saw an opportunity to expose corruption within the catering division. He claimed that all employees in the department were dishonest, suggesting that their duty records and health statuses needed to be scrutinised through rigorous medical examinations. Banfa's successor, however, was a man with strong political connections, and it became evident in the way he conducted himself, seemingly untouchable in his new role. Seizing any chance to downsize the staff, one of the military managing directors of the airline issued an order: every catering staff member had to undergo stringent medical tests at a private hospital handpicked by management.

Though the workers themselves did not initially question the testing, many suspected that the process might be rigged-perhaps the hospital was instructed to ensure that a certain number of employees would be deemed unfit to work in food processing. When the results came in, they were harsher than anyone anticipated. Nearly half of the catering staff were dismissed on medical grounds. The union made every effort to demand transparency in the testing process, but none of their requests gained approval.

Meanwhile, the airline was rapidly losing revenue, and the union feared that wages might not be paid in the near future. Concerned for both the short- and long-term survival of the airline, the union organised a bilateral conference, which was overseen by the Nigeria Labour Congress and the Trade Union Congress. At the conference, it was proposed that the catering division should be privatized. This would enable it to deliver high-quality food for both domestic airlines and international flights, which could pick up return journey menus from Lagos.

A detailed proposal was printed and submitted to the managing director of the airline, with a copy sent to the Minister of Aviation to ensure that the ministry overseeing the airline was aware of the plan. The union made it clear they were available for further discussions on short notice. But to their dismay, the management did not even acknowledge receipt of the report. Despite numerous follow-ups, it became evident that the document had been shelved without consideration. The opinions and suggestions of the workers, who had dedicated themselves to serving their country, were completely ignored.

What added to the union's frustration was the airline's financial misconduct. Records revealed that some members of the management team were withdrawing up to 2 million Naira weekly as part of an "IOU" scheme. This money was funnelled directly to the catering division, in collusion with several directors and the head of audit. At the time, the airline operated only one aircraft, which was frequently grounded due to technical issues, yet the weekly withdrawals continued unabated. The very individuals who were supposed to safeguard the airline's finances were the ones perpetrating the fraud.

Before any funds were released, the Director of Finance was required to sign off, ostensibly to confirm the legitimacy of the expenditure. But this process, too, was compromised. The Director of Human Resources, tasked with handling administrative matters and disciplining employees, ensured that any complaints or allegations from whistle-blowers were buried if they implicated him in the scheme. The third player in this network of corruption was the auditor, who reviewed all receipts. As long as his division refrained from filing any adverse reports, there was no alarm to alert others to the ongoing fraud. The system, tightly controlled from within, left little room for accountability or justice.

CHAPTER EIGHTEEN

THE DUTCH AIRLINE (KLM)

IN A BOLD and unexpected move, the Federal Government of Nigeria contracted the Dutch airline, KLM, to manage Nigeria Airways—a decision that sent shockwaves through the aviation industry and left many baffled. KLM, which had already established itself as a competitor to Nigeria Airways by operating international flights from London Heathrow and London City Airport to Nigeria via Amsterdam, suddenly found itself at the helm of the national carrier. This surprising development raised many questions: What were the commercial or operational advantages that prompted such a decision? What financial interests or debt reduction plans did the government hope to achieve by entrusting a foreign airline with the management of the country's national carrier?

For many, the decision seemed illogical and even reckless. The workers of Nigeria Airways were kept in the dark, unaware of the contract's details, the terms, or even whether a competitive tender process had taken place. Who had submitted proposals? What conditions had been stipulated? Why had KLM been chosen over other potential candidates? These unanswered questions cast a long shadow over the entire process. Since its inception in 1960, the management of Nigeria Airways has been plagued by inefficiencies, often driven by political favouritism rather than merit. Tribal and political allegiances frequently influenced the appointment of top management, leaving the airline in a state of disarray. But the notion of handing over the airline's reins to a foreign company as a solution to these internal issues seemed far from realistic—some even considered it an act of desperation.

KLM's takeover, however, was not without consequences. The Dutch airline was not only responsible for managing the day-to-day operations of Nigeria Airways but also for footing the salaries and allowances of its staff seconded to Nigeria. These salaries, often far higher than those of their Nigerian counterparts, strained the already ailing airline's finances. KLM pilots, flying DC-10s and Boeing 747s, earned vastly more than Nigeria Airways' pilots, exacerbating the disparity. While KLM may have had its reasons for seeking the contract, and while certain promises were likely made behind closed doors, the Nigerian public was left with only the official announcement: Nigeria Airways had been handed over to KLM to resolve its financial woes and return the airline to profitability. Yet, this "philosophical" vision—of reviving the airline through foreign management and eventually handing it back to Nigeria—was widely viewed as naive, a pipe dream destined for failure. It was as though the government had shot itself in the foot, deciding with far-reaching consequences but little hope of success.

When KLM was contracted to manage Nigeria Airways, the state of the national airline was grim. Most of its aircraft were grounded and rendered unserviceable due to a chronic lack of funds for essential spare parts. However, it wasn't a shortage of technical expertise that crippled the fleet; rather, it was the inability to maintain the planes. Some aircraft had been flown abroad for heavy maintenance, such as the ones serviced in Air Lingus hangars. However, delays in payment for parking charges had caused fees to soar, and as a result, these planes were left in Ireland, languishing until Nigeria Airways was eventually liquidated in 2003. This left a void in the fleet, one which KLM was quick to exploit. They stepped in, replacing the defunct aircraft with their planes and crews, operating on Nigeria Airways' routes and schedules, all while drawing payment from Nigeria Airways' accounts. These KLM-operated flights were immensely profitable, but for Nigeria, the tangible benefits were less clear—a question that continues to linger in the minds of many.

On the ground, KLM assumed control with subtle but significant changes. While the Nigerian directors kept their titles and salaries, KLM inserted themselves as "Directors-in-Charge" of key departments. Effectively, this created two tiers of leadership within each department—Nigerian directors who retained their roles in name only, and KLM directors who held real power. The former Nigerian directors found themselves sidelined, reduced to little more than figureheads who ran minor errands or followed directives from their new KLM bosses. A sense of confusion often pervaded the ranks, as employees were unsure whether to defer to the Nigerian director or the KLM-appointed leader. For example, during my time as the Administrative Officer in the Motor Transport division under the Engineering and Maintenance department, I found myself writing disciplinary letters on behalf of the KLM Director-in-Charge, while still having to copy the Nigerian director, whose role had diminished to little more than a bystander. Communication within the airline became layered and complex, with messages being routed through the Managing Director and eventually landing on the desks of KLM directors, who had the final say in most matters. Meanwhile, the Nigerian directors were consulted primarily on minor issues, especially those involving local political sensitivities. In essence, they became silent participants in the management of an airline that once belonged to them. WHAT A FUNNY SITUATION BUT VERY PECULIAR TO DRAW THE LINE OF SUPERIORITY.

When the KLM team arrived in Nigeria to manage the national carrier, Nigeria Airways, they brought with them a standard of living that matched what they were accustomed to in their home country. Rather than adjusting to the conditions of their new environment, their living standards were elevated to reflect their elite status. Nigeria Airways was compelled to rent large, fashionable houses in upscale locations for the KLM staff and their families, ensuring these homes mirrored the luxurious lifestyle they were used to. The absence of reliable electricity prompted the installation of heavy-duty diesel generators that ran 24/7. Additionally, water supply was an essential consideration. Each house was provided with 1,500 gallons of water daily to maintain their domestic needs and swimming pools. With no access to Nigeria Airways' boreholes, they resorted to purchasing water from private vendors, who, aware of the buyers' prestige, inflated

THE DUTCH AIRLINE (KLM)

their prices. The homes were furnished not with local goods but with imported furniture from Amsterdam, all at the expense of Nigeria Airways. KLM's role in the airline extended beyond housing—their directors took control of the company's financial decisions, with only speculation surrounding where the money truly went.

In an attempt to justify their contract, KLM proposed dividing Nigeria Airways into two entities: retaining the name for domestic flights while establishing "Air Nigeria" for international routes. They even constructed a new head office for Air Nigeria, equipped with the latest IT systems, but the equipment mysteriously began disappearing, with no investigations conducted. Despite this ambitious restructuring, the airline's financial situation worsened both domestically and internationally under KLM's management. The issues of flight delays, cancellations, and inefficiencies remained unresolved. KLM's personnel often opted to fly with private airlines, which offered earlier departures, leaving Nigeria Airways' planes idle until after 11:00 AM. Nigerian pilots, cabin crews, and engineers were left redundant, their skills underutilized, and their flight hours stagnating. When Nigeria Airways' planes developed minor issues, KLM quickly hired their aircraft, passing the costs, including crew accommodations at Sheraton Hotel, to Nigeria Airways. In the end, KLM's management contract yielded no meaningful improvements. The airline's debt swelled, and the opportunity for growth was squandered. What was supposed to be a partnership for revitalization instead became a burden, with KLM ultimately departing, leaving Nigeria Airways in a worse financial state than before. The blame, however, could not solely be placed on KLM; it was a consequence of poor governmental oversight and the misplaced belief that foreign intervention alone could solve internal problems.

CHAPTER NINETEEN

SALES OF BOEING F. 28 AIRCRAFT

THROUGHOUT THE HISTORY of vehicle manufacturing, accidents, whether involving motor vehicles or aircraft, have often been tied to human error or mechanical malfunction. Manufacturers, no matter how reliable, are not immune to such incidents. Take, for example, the case of Toyota, one of the most reputable names in the automotive industry, particularly known for the durability of its engines. At one point, Toyota was forced to recall millions of vehicles of a specific model after reports surfaced about mechanical faults. This decision, though costly, was crucial for maintaining the brand's strong reputation. The same principle has applied to aircraft manufacturers, who have occasionally faced issues with their planes, though not every problem result in mass recall or grounded fleets. However, when accidents become frequent or are linked to specific models, the international community demands investigations, and buyers and operators alike call for accountability. No airline or vehicle operator wants to be associated with incidents that risk lives.

One notable example of this took place with Nigeria Airways, which had acquired three Fokker F28 aircraft, highly praised for their low maintenance requirements and advanced technology that made them especially reliable in difficult weather conditions. Despite their stellar reputation, when one of these aircraft was involved in an accident during landing, the airline grounded the other two planes, even though there were no widespread reports from other operators indicating a manufacturer defect. This decision led to severe consequences: the planes deteriorated from lack of use, and the airline's crew, including pilots and cabin staff, faced underemployment or potential retraining. The loss of revenue for the airline was significant. Investigations later revealed that basic maintenance checks were often delayed due to internal management issues, including postponed purchases of essential spare parts. Eventually, the two grounded aircraft were sold at a significantly lower price than their value, a situation exacerbated by the long period of inactivity and the influence of opportunistic middlemen who prioritised their gain over the airline's financial interests. What could have been a routine operation recovery turned into a major financial and operational setback for Nigeria Airways, showcasing the far-reaching consequences of mismanagement and neglect.

The buyers of the aircraft may not have intended to use them for flight operations but saw an opportunity to make a quick profit by reselling them at a much higher price. For Nigeria Airways, the decision to sell the planes was simply to clear space in an overcrowded hangar. However, for many of the airline's engineers, the sale was a bitter blow. These aircraft were more than just machines;

they were cherished and admired, an integral part of their daily lives and expertise. These planes had become like family to the engineers, and the decision to sell them felt like a betrayal. But the wheels of bureaucracy had already turned, and the sale was finalized. For the airline's management, the priority was creating space, not the sale price. Yet, questions lingered—how much money had changed hands, and who benefited? In Nigeria, where such dealings are often shrouded in secrecy, nothing truly remains hidden for long.

Years later, word spread that one of the aircraft had been purchased by the Libyan government and repurposed as their Presidential jet. There were even whispers that during an official visit to Libya, the Nigerian Head of State was flown aboard that very plane. Libyan President Muammar Gaddafi reportedly joked that they were flying in a Nigerian aircraft, a remark that left the Nigerian leader smiling but silent, careful not to invite humiliation. Rather than returning to Nigeria to demand an investigation into how such a well-equipped and beloved aircraft could have been sold, the incident was quietly brushed aside. The Nigerian government and the airline's management chose to let sleeping dogs lie, avoiding the political fallout and media scrutiny that might have otherwise ensued. And so, the story faded into the background, just another chapter in the long history of decisions left unchallenged.

CHAPTER TWENTY

THE ANNUAL HAJJ OPERATIONS

THE HAJJ OPERATION was and still is an annual Muslim event in which devoted and dedicated Muslims worldwide congregate in the Holy lands of Mecca and Medina to perform the fifth Pilar of Islam Law which emphatically states and I quote, "Going to Mecca and Medina for those who have the financial capacity and the good health to undertake the pilgrimage". I am not presenting this book to interpret this pillar which is the fifth and the last of the most important instructions of our Prophet Mohammed in the life of a dedicated Muslim. No Muslim either well versed in the Quran or not has no ambition to see and pray in the Holy Land as it has become part and parcel of teaching and lecture that it helps you to enter into "Aljana" after departing this world on death. The annual event had been imbued by the Federal Government and has become a national issue to ensure the smooth operation in time of airlifting of the intended travellers to Saudi Arabia were arranged in a befitting accommodation and feeding for them, their health issues and uninterrupted airlifting back to the country after the pilgrimage was to the priority of the governments at the State and the Federal levels.

To achieve these enumerated objectives as stated above, the Federal government set up a national body called the Nigerian Muslim Pilgrimage Welfare Board (NMPWB) to give the body an executive power that would enable the body to perform its duties most judiciously, the Federal government enacted the National Hajj Commission (NAHCON) establishment ACT in 2006 to give an effective link to the government with the appointment of the executive chairman. The National Hajj Commission had a Welfare Board in each State of the Federation that coordinated the operation of their states and made regular reports to the NAHCON. The NAHCON made recommendations to the Federal Government as to the names of airlines that will carry out the lifting departures of people who have met the regulations set out in place by the central body in important areas of payment and meeting the medical requirements and the time the operation should commence and completed to meet the regulations of the host country. In every country where national interest was to be considered in which assignment that carries the image and reputation of the country are given top priority. That was the usual situation up to twenty years ago. The Federal Government used its stakeholder power to mandate the national airline to be the sole operator of the Hajj Operation since the Ministry of aviation is directly in control of the airline. On a few occasions, the airline struggled to carry out the duty without a hitch once the state governments had their arrangements efficiently set out and timetables announced to the states.

However, experience showed that there are always human errors concerning state arrangements. The Murtala Muhammed International Airport Lagos used to be the main departure tarmac for pilgrims from the South West of the country, and experience showed that the state representative of the state body must make arrangements for the road transportation of their travelling community to Lagos which always experience one hitch or the other. Most of the time, the passengers were never available to meet the airline arrangement as per scheduled departure; therefore, complaints, delays and other factors of criticism became the other of the day. Most travellers were ignorant of the principle of schedules and delays or cancellations caused by their state officials. All that concerned them was the issue of their not being taken to Saudi Arabia as promised.

The Federal Government spokesperson particularly the Minister of Information was never honest in the way and manner they presented their case to the public at large. They were been human beings who must protect the interest and image of the government by saying what favours the government and apportioning blame to other organisations. Everybody who has ever had causes to execute contracts with the government either as an individual, corporate body or parastatals must have experience on how easy it might be to get the contract, how difficult to source the finance to carry out the contract and how hazardous it becomes to get the payment for the delivered, signed for and collected that meet the required conditions without any form of complaint. Nigeria Airways was not different from what individuals through when it comes to the stage of payment for what they have obliged on behalf of the Federal government. Bearing in mind that because of the time factor involved in the airlifting. Most of the time, the national airline was often required to increase its fleet of aircraft by hiring on wet leases from foreign airlines which cost additional costs to the airline. We should understand that by the regulations governing either high purchase or hiring in all developed countries failures to pay due debts on the matured dates will attract compound rates of interest or legal proceedings which involve a legal team being hired and paid for.

The interest rate of buying an aircraft on high purchase contracts increases the price the buyer has to pay and a failure to pay when due was the foundation for the huge international debts that crippled both the Nigerian Airways and the Nigerian Ports Authority when their properties or valued items were seized round the world and because payment failed to be forthcoming the ships were sold in auction sales i.e. at a price to cover the debts upon which their property was seized. The constitution of Nigeria tells us that every citizen is equal before the law i.e. what applies to A should also apply to B and the right of A should be equal to the rights of B. This has ever been a common language, slang you hear on radio and television programmes promoting the cause of the government, that it is never backed up by any practicality. The idea that "man pass man" seemed to be the first line of our law of morality and the first paragraph of our constitution when it comes to practice.

Some influential politicians and business people who had strings they could pull or ears that could listen to their requirements started to influence the Federal government and they were consequently awarded the lifting of the people who were proceeding on the Hajj Operation. It soon became imperative that the national interest which could have been economically used to the advantage and progression of the national airline was diverted to the purse of the powerful and influential people who had no registered airline nor operated an airline. There should be no argument that anybody could be awarded the contract as both Nigerians and Nigeria parastatals. But what we used to see on the tarmac during the airlifting was a complete national disgrace and unimaginable. The winner had to hire foreign airlines to carry out the operation on behalf of the Federal Government or the Nigerian Pilgrimage Board. This book is not in a position to criticize the award of the contract nor how smooth or otherwise the operation was usually carried out. Such narration would attract criticism as injustice and bias. Those who are affected by the uphill situation will have to bear the brunt of what they went through many years after the years they tried to travel.

Africans in general had the culture of extended family, therefore, whenever we had the opportunity to travel outside our village, those who were aware that we were travelling would often or naturally ask us to buy something for them to make them always remember our journey or we took it upon ourselves to buy whatever we could afford for as many family members as possible, loved ones and friends to mark the occasion. The same principle applies to those people who are fortunate enough to have the resources in terms of finance and good health to proceed on the Hajj Pilgrimage to Mecca and Medina. Although the book of truth showed without doubt that most of them are sponsored by the Federal or State government for one service or the other on past political support, political sponsorship, and cronyism which showed that my townmate, my school mates and my constituency supporters must benefit and see my environment's hand works. Most of them at the time of departure always carry small parcels of bags which often contain one or two extra dresses that the welfare Board must have advised them are accepted and would serve a useful purpose when they were in Saudi Arabia. Some people also carry with them their cultural and traditional foodstuffs which would not be available in foreign countries as to what they learnt from people who had performed the Hajj in the past as a precaution of what to expect. Sometimes, if not most of the time, they have to hide it very closely as bringing it to Saudi Arabia could make it a criminal offence. Some of such goods are confiscated and thrown into the wasteland. It was not uncommon that, most food items smuggled to Saud Arabia were seized and destroyed by the host country as it contravenes what is allowed to their country. Some people were eventually issued with documented papers of warning to serve as a deterrent against another occasion.

After the Pilgrimage, most travellers used their foreign exchange which they had bought from Nigerian Banks when they were In Nigeria, they used the foreign currencies to go shopping with the additional foreign currencies they bought from the black markets called Bureau de change for shopping either for items for sales or for their family or as gifts for their friends or distant relations. Therefore, those who held one small parcel of a bag when they were departing Nigeria could become the owners of more than six or seven pieces of luggage per person. Therefore, their return journey becomes more complex and difficult to manage than at the time of departure from Nigeria. The new Alhajis and Alhajas would not want to pay excess money for the excess luggage as they would claim it was the responsibility of the airline or the government that sponsored them or conveyed them to the Holy Land to return them without any additional payment despite that their size of pieces of luggage had changed from the approved flight information.

Those who were conversant with the Hajj operation or read about it in the news media knew that the Federal government had to tackle a similar situation yearly on how to return the people to Nigeria with all their pieces of luggage as promptly as possible so that they could be with their families. The problem of left-over luggage did not concern the private people who politically acquired the contract of the operation by all means. The winners of the contract were found wanting as they only succeeded in repatriating sometimes about 75 per cent of the people and 10 per cent of their pieces of luggage most of the season. On the luggage left over in Jeddah and Medina virtually the Saudi authority was always issuing a strong circle of threats that they would destroy any luggage not taken away within two weeks after the Hajj had been completed.

For the Federal government to save face and with the greatest pressures from the Pilgrimage Welfare Board not to demean their status, the Federal Government often used their stakeholder power on the management of the national airline to make all the necessary flights in airlifting the abandoned passengers left over's pieces of luggage back to Nigeria. When the Minister issued such an instruction, no managing director of the national airline would carry out the order. There are records of some years when the national airline had to make as many as twenty airlift trips in a cargo plane to Saudi Arabia solely to bring back the abandoned passengers and the left-over pieces of luggage. This assignment was carried out at the appeal of the Federal Minister of Aviation. In doing this as part of the national assignment, the national airline had incurred expenses on aircraft fuel, and airspace in every country the aircraft flew over and had to paid landing, parking and use of ground operational equipment when they were loading the goods in Saudi Arabia. The government would not ask the person or company that won the contract and executed the contract shabbily or inconclusively to make the mandatory payment to the Nigeria Airways and the Minister on whose directive the flights were carried out the supportive assignments would not speed up the payments that the airline had tendered to the government to settle the bills. The managing director and Chief executive Officer who was in a political position to pursue the payments whether during the military or civilian regimes would rather prefer to protect their position of appointment than be vocal in pursuing such payments most judiciously. What this type of situation implied was that Nigeria Airways was the property of the Federal government and nobody cared whether it was paid for services rendered or not.

Let me just quote from the Nigerian Tribune publication of Saturday 27th May 2010- which categorically stated that the Ogun State Pilgrims were stranded in Saudi Arabia as the earmarked Med-View airline failed to complete the evacuation of the pilgrim return to Nigeria. It was also stated that Saudi Arabia had to save the face of the Nigerian government's international embarrassment by arranging an alternative airline by hiring Euro Atlantic airline to return the Ogun State contingent to Nigeria with the remaining Pilgrim Welfare officials who were stranded. The arrangement to evacuate people from the Holy Land after certain days of delay would attract a severe penalty and the number to be admitted from the country in the following year may be curtailed on the grounds of lack of proper and efficient management. If it were the time Nigeria Airways was in operation, it would be ordered by the Federal Minister of Aviation to instantly rescue such failure in completing the project. No official was prepared to state how many quantities of pieces of luggage were waiting for evacuation in the Holy Land.

Automatically, the Saudi Arabian authority would bill the Federal government for the hiring of the extra flights as they were not responsible for the return of the Pilgrims to their fatherland. If it was Nigeria Airways that was asked to undertake the assignment it would be charged for all facilities. Once the settlement failed to meet the standard payment procedures the airline would be charged a high rate of interest on the outstanding debts. The Federal government or the Nigerian Pilgrim Board would now be forced to pay up most urgently to save their reputation as failure to do so could have a serious repercussion against future relationships with the host country.

CHAPTER TWENTY-ONE

ABANDONED AIRCRAFT AT AIR LINGUS HANGER IN IRELAND

NIGERIA AIRWAYS USED to have one of the largest and most equipped aircraft hangers in Africa. The company devoted a reasonable proportion of their annual budget to providing training both within the country and at an internal level for its engineering workers. There was no grade of aircraft maintenance licence that Nigerian workers did not hold. It was a big competition between staff to ensure that you achieve the highest level of Licence. To make the completion very stiff and challenging, their contract of employment and Aviation regulations allow them to be catapulted from one level one plane to a higher level that measures with the technical licence they have just acquired through examinations.

This made most of the engineering staff spend their resources to action undergo professional courses privately while working but sometimes the most ambitious may take some months off duty without pay to prepare themselves in terms of reading and sitting for a series of examinations. Incidentally, their professional examination bodies in collaboration with AITA and ICAO did ensure an automatic upgrade into the newly acquired qualifications grade. As a Human Resources personnel staff, I have prepared upgrading papers for an engineering staff from grade level 07 to grade level 12 based on the newly acquired Frame Licence and the upgrading was instantly approved by the director of that department. Probably another department that had something similar with automatic upgrading then was the Pilots at the operation department of the airline. That made the staff in another department to be jealous of those exceptional facilities.

Many staff were sent on local and international training and seminars to meet the budgeted plans approved by the management. Therefore, Nigeria Airways spent a reasonable size of its budget to upgrade the staff and equipment in engineering and the Pilot to maintain very high standard of efficiency and make their staff current with the new developments in the aviation industry. When a new aircraft purchase is needed to be acquired, there is always provision for the manufacturer of the aircraft to provide essential maintenance courses, training and seminars for the staff of the buyers to be provided with maintenance procedures as part of the sales promotion and contracts.

Let us take the case of a particular aircraft the airline had recently purchased such as the Air-Bus, they were on high purchase as the airline could not afford their payments outright as did by the very rich and industrialised countries like the USA and Saudi Arabia and well-established airlines like Emirate and Qatar Air, the manufacturer financial Bankers or Institutions that would be guaranteed payment in case of default, it was important that the buyer must ensure that the aircraft is airworthy and all papers that will make it to fly to any country is an update. Most of the time, to generate revenue to pay for the agreed annual or monthly repayment with the required interest rate. The seller therefore will when occasion warrant in the term of the contract sends their expert staff to have an inspection whether the users' regulations were adhered to or not and often in a position to make useful suggestions as to how aircraft could most and maximum maintained to the benefit of both parties and attract other airline operators to be interested in the purchase of the aircraft.

Every aircraft has a catalogue of maintenance regulations such as at what mileage certain engineering checks must be carried out to avoid air disasters. In recent times, one of the Air Bus 308 planes purchased by Air Qantas of Australia had an engine crack that some part of the engine to fall off on flight in the air. This situation sent an urgent sign to all purchasers of the particular type to ground them for proper investigation and wait for manufacturer reports to see how serious and universal the problem may be similar in other aircraft If it was an isolated problem, the other aircraft will return into service with clearance and assurance from the manufacturer. Many grades of maintenance engineering works could be undertaken at Ikeja Technical services. By and large, the management failed the Technical Service by not providing most of the required equipment and facilities to meet the level of maintenance and repairs granted to the airline or that could utilise the academic potentialities of their licence engineer.

Annual budget proposals were an annual ritual in which each department deployed its technocrats to comply with what the department could aim to achieve in the following year. Like the national budget presented by the President of the country to the House of Senate and the House of Representatives for scrutinise, debate, analysis and subsequently approval after all the minuses and pluses have been made to reflect the objectives of the government, the Senate and the House of Representative through their Finance committees must show that observe and suffer in daily practical life hence people often they represent the people and still create havocs which may need compromise for the passage of the budget before it receives the Presidential signature which made it to become implementable. Approval and announcement through the annual budget broadcast do not reflect what the people observe and suffer in daily practical life hence people often wonder what were the reflection of the budget on their day-to-day experience.

Therefore, like the experience of the nation, the issue of an annual budget in the airline was also a ritual for the management to have all their activities incorporated into their annual reports to the Minister of Aviation. Both IATA and ICAO were very strict in granting licences for certain grades of maintenance of aircraft to airline operators to undertake certain levels of repairs and maintenance of check levels to be carried out at local hangers. Had the government provided all the required facilities, the maintenance department would have got all levels of manpower to maintain all the four grades of checks required in most aircraft. In Africa, the Ethiopian airline had met all the required conditions by the AITA and had already been granted such a licence. It is on record that Nigeria Airways sometimes fly their aircraft to Ethiopia hanger for crucial check D. Aircraft routine checks are divided into four

ABANDONED AIRCRAFT AT AIR LINGUS HANGER IN IRELAND

categories. Check A is the hourly check mostly on the engine of the aircraft after certain hours of flights. Like a diligent driver on the road, who checks the level of the battery liquid after a certain mileage to make sure the vehicle engine does not knock. Also, the radiator level of water that needs to be checked and the engine oil level as any deficiency in these materials could cause the car engine to knock out anytime and anywhere.

Similarly, as Nigeria Airways belongs to the government of Nigeria, the Ethiopian airline was owned and operated by the government of Ethiopia, and we could not make any comparison in the Gros National Product nor Capital per head of the two countries. Ethiopia is a completely desert country where the citizens and the national revenue are derived from arable agriculture. We have heard, read and seen on International Television News how the dry season had turned Ethiopia into a country that earned the lowest income in the Universe. During the reign of Emperor Hail Selassie, the Emperor of Africa as politically called him then and worshipped by the black race of the USA, West Indian States particularly in Jamaica were ravaged by Reggae music in his image. There was an area of comparison between Nigeria and Ethiopia apart from the image of each being a country or a nation to show their economic, political and structural independence and the right to be a member of both organisations of the African Union and United Nations. In size and population, in education and academic achievements, in GNP and CPH, Nigeria is supposed to stand far taller than Ethiopia in all areas which will make comparison not a matter of consideration. Most remarkable, corruption, lack of honesty, lack of dedication, lack of national interest, and lack of continuous and consistent planning from one regime of government to another either military or civilian, democratic or feudalistic had made Nigeria to be a move and stop nation which had impeded her economic prosperity.

It was a situation that caused a swell of shed of tears to those who are concerned about the political and economic lack of making any significant progress towards lack of actualisation in the pursuit of national developments. When Nigeria Airways with the blessings and approval of the Federal Ministry of Aviation had to sign a contract with the Ethiopia airline for the purpose of using the later engineering expertise to under the check D on Nigeria Airways aircraft due to accumulated international debts the national airline had incurred nearly round the universe became most ridiculous political and economic suicide Nigeria had ever committed. While Nigeria Airways had all the expertise, the licence personnel's, the hanger that was spacious enough to accommodate most aircrafts on the fleet of the airline, the government had failed woefully to provide the facilities and essential engineering tools to enable the international aviation supervisory body to grant the necessary licence to make the airline first of its kind in West Africa region of aviation industry in the region.

Ethiopia passed all requisite tests and supervisions that were required to be licenced to all stages of aircraft checks in their hangar. Nigeria Airways was reduced to the backstage where they had to fly their aircraft to Ethiopia for check D maintenance. Unfortunately, there was no record of how much Nigeria Airways owed the Ethiopia Airlines for the maintenance the airline has done for the national airline but speculatively, it could have run into millions of dollars. We are always shrewd in secret as diplomacy and confidentiality do not allow certain information to be splashed across the newspapers and other media as they do in developed countries. The Ministry of Information has ever been noted to cover up the release of information about the regime they were serving once it does not portray the government in their desire since they must be seen to be competent and capable of performing in their portfolios

Let me go to the particular area of this chapter that is most spectacular to the reader. Some years back before the liquidation of the Nigeria Airways, the airline was contracted by force and influence politically too powerful people too strong for the airline to resist or waive off. These powerful people jumped start the airline to negotiate for the competent aircraft maintenance firm that could undertake the repairs and servicing the major works on their two Boeing 707 cargo planes. The arrangement was the negotiation and the consequence signing of the contract was concluded before the airline could write out on their maintenance records sheet and what was to be done to negotiate which airline was most considerate standard-wise and coastwise for the job. The instruction came from the above that an arrangement had been concluded for the two aircraft to be flown to the Republic of Ireland Aer Lingus workshop for the D check. By the nature of the size and delicacy of the composition of aircraft and the distance they are to be taken to, they must be maintained and flown worthy to the country they were to be taken. The order from the highest authority which cannot be ignored nor disobeyed was duly complied with and the aircraft were flown down to the designated airport in Ireland.

Within a few days or weeks, the required jobs were thoroughly carried out, the aircraft were tested and found suitable to be returned to the owner. Nigeria Airways had no information as to the costs of the contract since there was no airline impute to the negotiation. Some fast middlemen assumed responsibility for the initiation and negotiation for the airline to carry out the maintenance. It became problematic and prolonged negotiation when the issue of payment for the maintenance reared its ugly head as it was conditioned that payment must be completed before they would be released to be flown back to the country. The Federal Ministry of Aviation promised heaven and to get ministerial approval for the Federal government to help in settling the bill. On several occasions, NIGERIA Airways sent their representatives to make occasional visits to Aer Lingus to monitor the jobs as they progressed from one stage to another stage. They always return to make progress reports to the management confirming that good jobs are been done and the aircraft are signed off as due to be returned to the operator.

It is not implied here that the costs of the maintenance carried out were deliberately or in deliberated inflated nor that the fast-middle class operators who made the necessary contracts and used their influence to obtain the necessary ministerial approval but when you read about the recent incidents were some contracts at some Nigerian airports runways were deliberately inflated by the ministers who persuaded the contractor in Austria to increase their quotations for their interest, it can be seen that some situation is impossible can only be found in the dictionary of a fool. I am using this information that is in the public domain and with the EFCC disposal. Have we forgotten the derogatory issue of Halliburton scam which the Federal government have not been bold enough to tell the nation and her citizens who are the people involved and by how much per person that was shared? As one person said, 'the Sharia law allows the hand of a person who stole a purse or chicken to be cut off while the lawmakers, the Bank directors and the governors who made the laws for us and execute them could get away unpunished when they have glaringly stolen trillions of people money given to them to improve the live hood of the people.

I could remember vividly and as if it was recorded video or DVD, the situation I found myself in when I first arrived at the Murtala Muhammed International Airport wing in 1979 after some years of absence from the country. For the first two hours that we disembarked, I was asking people when are we going to continue our journey to Lagos, because I found myself in an unimaginable state very difficult for me to assume we were in Lagos. The airport was extremely neat, the airport structure was unusual and not African-like, and the atmosphere inside the building was cool similar to what is obtainable in the country I have left behind in the country of my departure which is the United Kingdom. Fortunately, I was employed some months later closest to the same airport and had the sorrowful tales of watching the airport deteriorate to abysmal. The air conditioners used 24/7 were subsequently broken down due to lack of good maintenance or improper maintenance, since they could not be serviced efficiently locally the air conditioners were dismantled and airfreighted back to the original place of manufacture which was Italy. To ordinary people or in the interest of business, there should have been a maintenance agreement to the company that made the buying contract that should guaranteed regular maintenance and functioning but it is assumed there was nothing like such an agreement or the person who won the contract was a political bigwig that nobody could question. It became known in every nook and corner of the airport that the service was successfully done but there were two impediments, the first was that the NAA could not pay for the cost of the repair and maintenance in foreign currency and no promissory note would be honoured given the nature of the country's reputation, hence without full payment, one cannot remove the repaired air conditioners. The second story as reported in the tabloid newspapers of the country was that there was no sizeable aircraft to repatriate it back to Lagos. The authority has forgotten that Nigeria could ask, how the air conditioners managed to get to Italy. That is the issue with the government. At this point for diplomatic purposes, I will coin the language of the Lawyers when proceeding with a court case and they complete their submissions, they would say, "My Lord I rest my case". Let us allow a sleeping dog to lie down peacefully.

To go back to our original finding on the aircraft in Aer Lingus, several years after the aircraft works were completed, the aircraft was test-flown and ready to return to the country. It is very sad to mention that up to date, the aircraft had become a working locker for the Aer Lingus engineers to hang their working uniforms and tools and to serve as storage. Whenever any Nigerian is chanced to go to the Republic of Ireland. try to visit the Aer Lingus hanger and see for yourself the DE tolerated and a shed the aircraft which were flown from Lagos to that country had become. Where is our pride and where are our nationalistic ideologies? What do we want to rebrand and which angle of our national damaged image do we want to rebrand? Let the Minister of Information and Communication as it is now renamed tell the nation where do we go from here?

CHAPTER TWENTY-TWO

DECEMBER RETRENCHMENT TRAUMA

IT WAS ONCE said, "Cowards die many times before their death but the valiant never taste of death but once, death was said to be a necessary end and it will come when it will come". So, says in the book of Shakespeare at the assassination of Julius Caesar. In Nigeria Airways virtually all the staff became cowards and delusion when the end of the year steps into December, when it became obvious to some that Nigeria Airways would be swept away with the tide of retrenchment, some will survive but it was a tradition to go through the same vegetable state at the same period the following year. What were the virtues of December the last month of every year, the month our Lord Jesus Christ was born and his birthday was celebrated with fanfare around the world when special lights were switched on at commercial areas to attract buyers of goods and services. All sorts of assorted decorations were on display. Homes are booming with laughter and people are buying gifts of interest for their wives, husbands, lovers and children as signs of love. Wives are writing down the items they want to prepare for their family members as delicious menus. High Street shops reduced prices to attract both the regular and the new customers. That is the time gifts are exchanged as a gesture of true love. The time families and friends exchange visits and people have high hopes and plans for the oncoming New Year.

With the life we lived and worked then in Nigeria Airways, we are made to experience the opposite lifestyle completely different from what was narrated in the first paragraph above. We had the experience of opposite moods and expectations in our lives and those of our families were nothing to write home about. It had become traditional and customary for those who are honest and open-minded with their loved ones to inform them that anything can happen to their employment at their place of work. That was an indication that bad news might replace the joy other workers are looking forward in other organisations to bring back or make their relations look forward to.

The aura of retrenchment started almost every October after a management meeting decisions are taken as to what level of workforce that airline's financial capacity could accommodate in their annual budget. Secondly, management also decides what level of manpower each Department should be, hence the number to be weeded out or shelved had at that stage agreed upon. To formalise this decision, the managing director would write a top secret and confidential memo to the director of Human Resources to ask all departments to submit the list of names of people who shall be on the list of people to be retrenched from the services by the 30th of November. There is nothing that remains secret or confidential forever. Every procedure has to be carried out by human beings and in this instance by workers of the airline, not by a hired external contractor where people in one department have friends, relations or are connected socially to each other under having some common interest either as a member of the trade union, member of the thrift and co-operative, member of the Sky power Social Club or their families have met on few occasions and formed an association of common interest. Therefore, nothing goes under the carpet of secrecy or confidentiality for a long time. To avoid leakage of the list getting out of exclusiveness and causing riot, the head of the panel coordinating the retrenchment often warned the groups of people he selected to work with him that they must not mention or discuss names with anybody and if one of them is suspected or reported to be leaking information, he or she would be dismissed without an option of disciplinary procedures.

The procedures of retrenchment were exclusively secret and close almost to the conclusion once the directive got to the table of the Director of Human Resources. The Director had to single out one of his / her deputies and call Controllers to handle the matter to a conclusion. By records, no woman has ever been selected to do the horrendous services because women could easily break down when they see their friend's names or their staff on the list to be executed. Secondly, the assignment involved working at night for unpredictable periods, which is never convenient for married women with children. Nigeria is a country where a husband cannot trust their wives if she says she has been given a task that will make her stay in the office every night for an unpredictable time. This involved selecting a group of people that would collect the files of those workers whose directors had enlisted be leave the company.

The purpose was to check if there were any criminal or disciplinary records recorded in the file of the person listed to justify being retained in the list or a defence may be sent back to the director to give the person a second thought on why that person should be reconsidered. All that was a mere formality because the programme was to reduce the number of workers by a certain percentage which has nothing to do with previous offences, queries and warnings. Imagine a worker who had received letters of commendation for good performances recently or on several occasions but because his head of section or division does not like him or her for whatever reason may list his name for retrenchment or somebody who had just saved the airline from fraud or rendered a remarkable service should not be laid off instead should be commended and compensated or rewarded with upgrading. It doesn't work that way.

Therefore, once the group of secret operators were selected and briefed on their new mandate and assignment of operations, within a few weeks, they would be unplugged from their normal duties and from their normal section to an ad-hoc committee, you will find some people who are usually friendly and conversational becoming moody, incommunicado and disassociating or disengaging themselves from all social activities suddenly. Secondly, someone who used to come to work regularly, and be punctual at his desk every blessed day of the week suddenly came to work when other workers had closed for the day and were preparing to close from work and they were going home. The reverse was the case in the morning while the majority of the people were arriving for work, they were seen going home. That is the cause of suspicion that something is in the oven and everybody's minds go to the havoc of mass retrenchment. Finally, to keep their operation top secret, they were forbidden to be seen at the Sky Power Social Club so that they would not be intoxicated with drink and divulge information under the influence of alcohol.

These are the first signs that workers usually noticed before rumours started to gather storms about the impending lay-off of workers. During working hours, those who are observant could notice the movement of some individuals carrying out such voluminous size of files from the normal shelves and lockers to another office ferrying the files going in one direction and never returning for other users to have access to them. After work, people meet at the Sky Power Social Club where there is free speech and free interaction but, on this issue, when under discussion it is always a whisper and under-the-table talks. People will always conclude their discussions with such remarks as, "Please don't let any other person hear about this information, let me enjoy today as I don't know what may happen to the job tomorrow." Sometimes when your name is listed and some people with whom you used to joke loudly and share a rapport see you coming, they might have been talking about your situation, once they see you coming, by the time you get close to them they would change the topic all you will hear would be, " What was I talking about before", that should be seen as a sign of warning that your position may be at danger.

Let us look specifically at one particular December year retrenchment scenario during the tenure in office of Brigadier-General Oluyemi Omokuwajo Bajowa (rtd), he was the managing director of the airline when (3,600) three thousand six hundred workers were retrenched at a sweep throughout the airline network but mostly in Ikeja, the headquarters of the national airline. Mr M (to keep his name that way), was selected as the head of the panel for the exercise. From day one, he was appointed, but because the appointment was not publicised, it became glaring that he had assumed a secret assignment as he became invincible on his chair during the normal working hours of 08:00 to 16:00 hours as he was well known to be a man who was very punctual and was as constant as northern stars during office hours, both punctuality and his ethnic friends who were always visiting him as he was one of the advocate and propagandist for Ahioma State in Nigeria, they were agitating to be created out of the present Delta State, could no longer congregate in his office as usual to air their suggestions for the actualisation of their political dream as usual and they could not get him on both home and office phone numbers. Subsequently, he was leaving the office as early as 07:00 with his selected team workers while other normal workers were coming to the office to resume their normal duties.

Because of the volume of people on the list, the job was never an easy assignment. As much as they tried to keep the exercise under wrap, rumours started to fly over every nuke and corner of the company premises and people became worried as nobody could be sure or vouch for his employment after the exercise. Sky Power Social Club became a very crowded place where we organise together in terms of self-send-off. People got together section by section to treat themselves to a lavish dinner and drink to drown their sorrow of the impending bombshell of retirement and retrenchment. Departments were not exempted as the whole organisation was not fully productive in terms of productivity.

People who are not sure of their future guarantee of work cannot be expected to concentrate on their day-to-day work as everybody deserves assurance of permanent and secured employment which is no longer in existence.

The collation was completed and sent to the managing director for his approval which was channelled with priority. Two weeks before Christmas, rumours were flying in the air that with every breathable oxygen that people in the airline could inhale, workers were, almost if not virtually paralysed. Anywhere you go, the voice in every mouth was the impending retrenchment. There are two issues at stake, nobody was sure of the number of staff at stake, that were pencilled to go and there was an argument and counterargument about the department that might be most affected. In the process, we learnt that some directors were able to argue most vigorously in defence of the number of people allocated for retrenchment in that department, ironically, workers in Human Resources were said to be the highest in number on the list. This was influenced by a remark credited to one of the renowned, well-known and well-connected Pilot Captains who defended the mass removal of the people from human resources by saying that the airline does not need the present strength of staff in the personnel because the pilots could work out the hours of flying hours they did and multiply the current rate they were on and get paid. Secondly, their promotion or upgrading from one level to another does not need much processing and all the administrative stages their files pass through as they were prepared to affect a more straightforward formula to run their affairs was a waste of money.

What an ignoramus and share pomposity without regard for record-keeping and the management must have bought the idea without considering the future implications and complications. Some of the pilots who are school certificate failures but were admitted for pilot courses because they came from minority areas of the country or they were taken to complement the State quota system became so arrogant and looked down on other workers in other departments who have spent most of their useful year life to be highly educated and to attain their present grade level and status. What are the factors that made the pilot so tick and above the board? By the nature of their basic training, before they could be licenced as pilots, they must score up to 95 per cent in their courses. Candidates only need the basic GCE or West African Examination Council (WAEC) in probable mathematics and other two science subjects. Once you are privileged to be taken by an airline as a commercial pilot, all the requisite qualifications and training are the responsibility of your employers. But the joy of the profession is first to be called an aviation pilot and secondly, you fly from one airport to another airport within the country. Thirdly, once you become a senior flight officer, you could be attached to a bigger aircraft which flies from one country to another country called international flights and their financial rewards are multiple.

First is the privilege of being attached an extra flights and overnight allowances which enable them to possess flashy and expensive cars and be able to build houses of special designs in pushy locations. Secondly, those who are business-minded could buy sellable items for their wives' shops and make some profits to raise their standard of living and status in the community. While some of them are very humble and humane, realising that their position is an opportunity which is impossible for everybody to have, there are some of the pilots who allow the riches to enter into their heads and they sometimes talk, behave and have the attitude like a semi-god. Anyway, it is human to misconstrue one position or manner in life. Ironically, we could see some of the previously flamboyant captains of the 1970s and 1980s who came to the Sky Power Club and you could see that the sparkle, the glorious esteem and the untouchable phenomenon have either completely gone or it has mellowed to the ordinary level. That was why the wise man said, "Be good to the people you meet on your way up as you are likely to meet them, on your way down".

To reconnect where we diverged, exactly one week before the Christmas break, it became clear that Friday was the date earmarked that the staff of the airline had with faith. Between the hours of 08:00 and 12:00, all staff were sitting at the edge of their seats. You would be most embarrassed if you should enter another office to check for any action on whatever request you have sent there previously. Some men were even able to crack occasional jokes but the situation of women was completely pathetic. If I was chanced to enter into their brain, their problem must be related to how do I tell my husband and my children that I have lost my employment without committing any disciplinary offence, and for those with young children, how could they explain to them that they could not provide them with the usual Christmas and New Year treats they have done in the previous years. It was a dilemma without resolution. The fear was written on the faces of everybody. Whenever somebody knocked on the door to your office to come in, you could hear everybody sighing as if the person would produce a register and ask you to sign for your letter of retrenchment. The situation was so traumatic beyond description that some women were rushed by the company ambulance to the company health clinic for respiratory treatment. The situation was so beyond description, it was next to horror films. People collapsed and some fainted to show the gravity of the perplexing situation.

When my table phone rang, I was afraid to pick it up as who knows what news will come out of the other end. Incidentally, it was from my Divisional boss who asked me to report to her office "now". Before I left the office as other staff had done previously, I cleared my table and everything personal was already in a box which I could easily pick up to my car as my last walk out of the office as the staff of the airline and people who have worked with me for over six years. Before I stepped out, I told other staff that I had been called probably to come and collect my letter and that increased the tension and blood pressure and shiver of the rest of my staff. A walk which used to take me 5 minutes took me more than 15 minutes to her office within the same perimeters and I almost entered a wrong office as I could not get myself together. It is very sad when one loses concentration and it could result in heart failure, stroke, or heart attack if it is continuous over a while.

The preacher's sermon that one should be optimistic that it would and must be well in respect of the situation one had gone out of the window in most people's faith. It was a serious devastation and panic with unpredictability. When I got to the Madam's office, she gave me enough envelopes that were the same as the number of the staff in my section and asked me to sign for them.

As nature cannot be cheated, the first envelope I looked for was the one where my name was written but incidentally, it was not among. As she asked me to sign for them and allow her to deal with others because I was wasting her time, my hands became so frozen like somebody who had been inside the snowy winter for hours without gloves and with only a shirt and trousers as a dress without a pocket to keep the hands warm. My right hand was so shaking like somebody who was suffering from Parkinson's disease. When I signed for them, one spirit just took over me and I dared to ask her why she did not give me my letter at the same time so that I would not need to come back to the same office and see the others with perplexed faces. Just imagine her reply, "You go and distribute these letters first and then I will call you back when I am prepared to give you your own". "It was already in my drawer hence You don't need to be in haste, everybody knows you are a union man." What brought out my union affiliation was beyond my imagination and could not see the relevance to the issue at stake.

With the letters in my hands, I became perplexed and just stood there in one corner of the office of the fabricated building in Obi Village. I could not remember how long I was gummed to the floor and I could not remember that some people who were passing were saying something to me most of them with gloomy and wet faces of tears, but I was completely lost in thoughts and almost in spirit. By the time I realised that there was nothing I could do to rewind or reverse the situation, I must have spent about 30 minutes of very precious time but devastating time. I finally walked out but took a position by the corner of the long corridor. It must have been one of my staff who was looking for me as I failed to return in time that asked me what I was doing there before my mind woke up and I sluggishly came back to my office.

As I entered the office, I calmed everybody down by saying that we had all been retrenched and the office was completely closed down. Only one lady called Bola, one of the clerks dared to announce to the hearing of others that "Life must still continue and that Nigeria Airways is where we all come and we have to go one day". She concluded in Yoruba proverb, "Office ni oma rehin akowe". That statement and pronouncement just woke up the spirit of everybody and without protest and argument, everybody majestically signed their papers and we started hugging one another and after a few minutes, everybody started to move out with their personal effects on their hands and shoulders. What a devastating situation and it remained in my memory like a recorded DVD up to date. When people you are older than in age, senior in rank in office, and who have been looking unto you for their livelihood and upward uplifting of themselves and that of their families suddenly lost their jobs for no error or contributory disciplinary records, it was most traumatic and unspeakable. My grace was that they knew I was not a contributor directly or indirectly to the situation they found themselves in. It was done and dusted without my knowledge.

About two hours later in the day, I went back to Madam's office to collect my letter as she had pronounced. The premises had become a state of pandemonium and Policemen had been invited to take positions in strategic places to put the premises under law and order and to avoid acrimony. When she saw me approaching her office, she left her seat to meet me at the doorsteps. As if it was a pre-recorded tape, she told me to go back to the Mailing Office that with immediate effect all the remaining staff in that section should move and join my section as part of the new arrangements and by the end of the day which remained about two hours, I should come and tell her that all arrangements are on the desk so that the new office will start functioning on Monday. I was gruesome and speechless. She was sweating as if she was given orders to this and to that as her office entrance was barricaded by the Policemen and women were dressed in battle gear.

At about 4 pm, Mr M. who supervised and co-ordinated the exercise drove to the compound of the company, as one theorist put it probably to see part of the chaos the retrenchment had caused on the premises or as another theorist had put it, the office of the managing director might have called him on the phone that the MD will like to see him. He might have assumed he was called in for a thank you handshake for a job well executed which was difficult to substantiate except he had done what the management had desired. But according to most people's expectations, at about 19.30 when the office building had almost become empty, there was a phone call from the office of the managing director inviting Mr M. to see him for a consultation. Only God knows what transpired between the two people as he was only ushered in by the secretary to see the boss in the inner office while the door was closed firmly, but to the greatest dismay of the people who were still outside the Airways House at the time he walked out of the Airways House, Mr M. came out with a similar letter he had coordinated to others, he was said to be seriously confused, red-faced and his walking became unbalanced and could not look forward straight. He was holding an envelope of a letter personally signed by the managing director. Instead of smiles, he looked so glued and rumours had it that he actually missed one of the steps of the stairs and nearly fell if not for the Policemen who rushed to his aid when he was getting out of the Air House. Instead of being given a higher position of Director as a personal appreciation of the efforts he had expended into the task, instead of being shaken and seen out of the office as a sign of appreciation, instead of being hailed as a hero for his sacrifice of services to the management, as he was signing the retrenchment letters of mass of the people so also someone had signed Mr M letter and the letter was kept in the managing director drawer for the later date.

In Nigeria Airways, wonders know no end. Only those who were spared could live to tell the story, luckily, I was one of the survivors by miracle on several occasions of impediments.

CHAPTER TWENTY-THREE

INHUMANITY AT WORKPLACE

THE NIGERIAN CONSTITUTION stipulates that the government must treat all citizens equally and humanely, without discrimination, ensuring fairness for every individual with legal residency. This principle aligns with Nigeria's commitment to international conventions, especially the United Nations Human Rights Declaration, to which the country is a signatory. However, such promises often appear as lofty ideals, included to satisfy global standards, while their practical implementation remains a complex issue.

Nigeria Airways, the country's national carrier, is a key example of how these constitutional values were tested. Like any airline, Nigeria Airways was responsible for moving people across borders, requiring a vast network of employees both within Nigeria and abroad. To manage the operations abroad, the airline often hires locally in other countries. Familiar workers with the host nation's work culture and regulations are employed. These employees were referred to as "local staff."

For the most part, the airline's obligations to local staff were minimal. Their welfare fell under the jurisdiction of the host country, meaning the airline needed to comply with local laws regarding salaries, working conditions, and employment rights. For instance, foreign staff need appropriate visas, work permits, and accommodation. There were stringent laws about minimum wage, health and safety, and even the freedom to join trade unions. Violating these regulations could result in fines or legal actions against the airline. Despite being employed by Nigeria Airways, local workers had the right to seek legal recourse in their host countries if unfairly dismissed, similar to their native counterparts.

The airline's operations were expensive, with Nigerian staff being sent abroad as representatives of the company. When Nigeria Airways functioned at its peak, resources were regularly sent from Nigeria to pay staff overseas. This often involved converting Nigerian currency into foreign currency—like dollars or pounds—due to insufficient revenue generation abroad to cover costs.

However, as with many state-owned enterprises, the airline faced financial difficulties and eventually collapsed in 2003. Its assets were liquidated, and several properties, such as the Nigeria Airways House, were handed over to private firms like Arik Air. The once-busy premises of Nigeria Airways were reduced to a mere shadow of their former selves, now occupied by street vendors and currency traders.

The collapse of Nigeria Airways highlighted the stark difference between employee rights in Nigeria and those abroad. While foreign staff had the protection of their host country's laws, Nigerian employees had no such safety net. The process of retrenching staff was chaotic and poorly regulated. Unlike international companies like Pfizer, which ensured employees received their final paycheques and benefits immediately upon retrenchment, Nigeria's system lacked such provisions. Workers would often be handed termination letters without any arrangement for immediate payment, leaving them vulnerable and without recourse.

In reputable firms, the termination process is carefully managed. Employees are not only given a termination letter but also a final paycheque, including gratuities and pension entitlements. In Nigeria, however, retrenched workers had no such guarantees. The lack of laws protecting workers' rights in case of mass layoffs, particularly during Nigeria Airways' liquidation, left many employees struggling to claim their rightful dues.

The liquidation process further exposed the weaknesses in Nigeria's labour laws. Many employees were left in limbo because there were no clear legal frameworks mandating companies to pay retrenched workers promptly. This lack of transparency and accountability in the process, combined with the absence of strong worker protections, subjected workers to be at the mercy of their employers. This stands in stark contrast to countries like the UK, where strict employment laws ensure that workers are treated fairly during redundancies, with clear guidelines on wages, health and safety, and fair treatment.

Nigeria's employment laws, shaped by the legacy of military rule and decrees like those introduced by General Murtala Muhammed, have long failed to provide sufficient protection for workers. Under these decrees, retrenchments could not be challenged in civil courts, leaving workers with little to no legal recourse. Successive governments have maintained these laws, further eroding employee rights and leaving workers unprotected in an ever-shifting economic landscape.

The story of Nigeria Airways is more than just the rise and fall of a national carrier. It is a reflection of the challenges faced by Nigerian workers, who continue to grapple with inadequate labour protections and a system that favours employers over employees. While foreign workers enjoyed the protections of their host countries, Nigerian employees were left to navigate a complex and often unfair system that placed little value on their rights and contributions.

In the era of President Olusegun Aremu Obasanjo, a former military head of state who became Nigeria's first civilian president under the new democratic dispensation, Nigeria Airways met a tragic fate. The airline was liquidated, and with its collapse, thousands of workers were plunged into despair. These employees, many of whom had dedicated decades of service to the company, found themselves abandoned. There had been no provision for their entitlements, no safety net for when the company folded. The future they had built for themselves unravelled.

Some workers, once residents of bustling Lagos, were forced to retreat to their ancestral villages—places they had left behind decades earlier in pursuit of a better life. For many, their children had only known these villages as a place to visit during the holidays, but now it was their only refuge. The return was not voluntary; it was a journey back to a life they were no longer familiar with, a culture their children could barely understand, and a way of living that had become alien. The very places they had long forsaken now became their forced havens, all because they could no longer afford to pay rent in Lagos.

Critics might argue that these workers had simply returned to their roots, where their parents once lived. But life in the villages had changed dramatically, and the lifestyle these workers had known in Lagos was vastly different from that of their parents' time. The displacement was not just geographical—it was cultural, social, and emotional.

In a twist of irony, workers employed abroad—whether in the UK, the United States, or Europe—faced a much more favourable outcome. Owing to the strict employment laws in these countries, Nigeria Airways and the Nigerian government were forced to pay them their full entitlements. Failure to comply would have resulted in costly litigation that could have further embarrassed the government. British and American media, known for sensationalizing stories about Nigeria, would have jumped on the opportunity to report the scandal with all its exaggerated flair, potentially leading to political and economic sanctions. To avoid this, workers abroad were compensated between £20,000 and £80,000, depending on their years of service and position. But back home in Nigeria, the story was entirely different.

The Nigerian workers were neglected, left at the mercy of liquidators who seemed more interested in their gain than in the welfare of those they were meant to serve. The process was a nightmare. Workers were made to visit offices repeatedly, with no clear information on the documentation required to claim their entitlements. The suffering of these workers became a stark reflection of a popular saying in Nigeria: "When one Nigerian suffers, it is the joy of others with the power to solve their problems."

As the months passed, these once-proud employees found themselves spiralling into poverty. Some who had served the airline for over 30 years were now unable to afford rent. Families who once enjoyed regular meals and sent their children to good schools were now barely able to survive. School fees went unpaid, forcing children out of school at all levels—nursery, primary, secondary, and even university. Social activities that had once been a source of joy—family gatherings, town meetings, charity events—became a painful reminder of what they had lost. The fall from grace was swift and brutal.

In 2009, the former workers were summoned to verify their documentation for the payment of some arrears. It was an event that many would never want to relive. By then, countless workers had already passed away, unable to afford the medical treatment that might have saved their lives. Some arrived at the verification centre in ambulances, their bodies frail and emaciated. One heartbreaking sight was that of a former staff member being carried by his daughter, as though he were a child. Others were brought in wheelbarrows because their families could not afford to hire transport. These scenes drew crowds, as onlookers stared in disbelief at the skeletal figures of people who had once been robust and full of life.

The hardships extended beyond the workers. Their children, who once thrived in school, were now confused and disillusioned, wondering how the country their parents had served for so long could abandon them. Some parents, desperate to keep their children in school, sold their homes to cover tuition fees, only to find that upon graduation, there were no jobs for their children to take up.

As Nigeria's economic woes deepened, factories that once provided employment began relocating to neighbouring countries like Ghana, where conditions were more favourable. Even the electricity crisis contributed to the decline. By 2010, it had become common for every room in a shared Lagos apartment to have its generator, as the national power grid remained unreliable. The situation became so unbearable that even during festive seasons, like Christmas and New Year, some Nigerians opted to travel to Ghana just to escape the noise of generators and incessant fireworks. The once-celebratory sounds of the season had become another source of stress, as churches and mosques competed to draw worshippers with the loudest speakers, adding to the cacophony of daily life.

The fall of Nigeria Airways was not just the collapse of a company—it was the collapse of dreams, hopes, and livelihoods for thousands of Nigerians. The workers who had once proudly served the airline found themselves trapped in a cycle of poverty, unable to reclaim the life they had once known. Their suffering became a reflection of a nation that had failed to protect its own. Imagine trying to find peace and holiness amid such turmoil. How could anyone aspire to be a saint under these circumstances? Worship is a personal matter, a sacred connection between the soul and God. Yet, using religion as an excuse to disturb the peace of others, forcing sleepless nights upon them goes against the very essence of faith. People who work late in their offices deserve the peace of mind to rest and wake up as per their routines without being subjected to the noise of generators or abrupt calls for worship throughout the night.

El-Rufai, once the minister of the Federal Capital Territory and later governor of Kaduna State, made a sharp observation. In Nigeria, those in wealthy areas like Ikoyi and Victoria Island enjoyed uninterrupted electricity, but they didn't fully pay for the privilege. Meanwhile, the poor in places like Ajegunle and Mile 2 were extorted and harassed by the Power Holding Company of Nigeria (PHCN).

My personal experience with Nigeria's electricity system, though little in the grand scheme of things, was profoundly frustrating. I paid ₦50,000 for a pre-paid meter two years ago, only to be told the price had jumped to ₦85,000 and then to ₦110,000. Each time, officials from PHCN came to my home threatening to disconnect my service, ignoring the receipt I'd posted visibly on my gate. They had to be "settled"—such is the cost of being a Nigerian. This story, though seemingly unrelated, reflects a larger issue. Corruption in Nigeria's institutions often leads to the downfall of certain organisations while benefiting others with political or financial connections. The liquidation of Nigeria Airways, for instance, was not an isolated event. The assets were swiftly absorbed into companies where powerful individuals had vested interests.

Everyone in Nigeria faces different struggles at work. I consider myself fortunate. The positions I held in Nigeria Airways were precarious and could have easily led to my dismissal. Yet, somehow, I managed to survive. My journey began on the day I was hired, July 7, 1979. My first encounter with my boss was discouraging—he wanted to post me somewhere so difficult that I would either quit or be fired within three months. As I overheard his conversation, anger and anxiety swelled within me. But an elderly secretary saved me with wise words, urging me to remain calm and show self-control.

Despite my boss' clear disdain, he assigned me to the mailing section. It was a hazardous environment where every staff member seemed subservient to the whims of management. One particular Monday, after organizing the weekend roster, I found myself facing airport security. A parcel of Indian hemp had been found on a flight, and they demanded the names of the workers on the Sunday shift. When I reported the situation to my boss, his reaction was cold: "Didn't I tell you that you'd be in trouble? You should resign before you're dismissed." With no support from him, I handed over the men for investigation.

Challenges followed me everywhere. One afternoon, after an administrative officer fled in fear after discovering a juju spell left on his chair, my boss decided to transfer me to his position in the Motor Transport section. He thought it was good luck for me to go, hoping something bad would happen. Despite my efforts to avoid the posting, I was forced to accept the role. I even managed to allocate a company car to the same boss who had wished ill upon me, transforming the section despite his efforts to push me out. Eventually, my connections within the company helped block one of his attempts to transfer me again.

In my final years with Nigeria Airways, I took on more responsibilities—overseeing the cleaners, managing staff ID cards, allocating company housing, and arranging protocol for visiting flight crews. Handling international crews was particularly sensitive, as it involved securing accommodation in top hotels like Sheraton. Time was always against me. I had to secure funds in foreign currency, often carrying urgent letters from one department to another, facing ridicule and mistreatment along the way.

Audit staff even accused me of returning unspent dollars, suggesting we split the surplus. But I knew it was a trap, so I continued to document every transaction with meticulous care. Despite the insults and suspicion, I never faltered. Working for Nigeria Airways was a mix of adversity and perseverance. From the pilots who viewed themselves as elite, indifferent to the struggles of ordinary workers, to the arrogant captain who tried to dominate the Lawn Tennis committee, every day brought new challenges. But through it all, I managed to keep my footing, never allowing the negativity to overwhelm me.

In the end, this was my story. A man navigating the trials of a workplace rife with politics, egos, and corruption. Yet through discipline, patience, and faith, I survived. And that, perhaps, is the true lesson: that in a land full of obstacles, one must learn to rise above, for failure to do so can lead to far-reaching consequences—not just for the individual, but for the entire organisation.

BUT NIGERIA IS
MY COUNTRY

CHAPTER TWENTY-FOUR

NIGERIA AIRWAYS ACCIDENT RECORDS

AIRCRAFT ACCIDENTS THROUGHOUT history have been categorized into two main types. The first type occurs when the aircraft is still on the ground, often resulting in damage to the aircraft's body, potentially rendering it unflyable. These accidents frequently involve airport equipment like stair ladders used for boarding, loading vehicles transporting passengers to the tarmac, or refuelling trucks. Incidents involving such equipment were not uncommon, prompting organisations like the Federal Airports Authority of Nigeria (FAAN), previously known as the Nigeria Airports Authority (NAA), to provide extensive training for ground staff operating these vehicles. When accidents of this kind occurred, they often led to flight delays or cancellations. In some cases, the aircraft would incur landing charges for its extended stay at the airport. Fortunately, these accidents rarely resulted in fatalities, although minor injuries to the ground handler involved were not unheard of.

The second type of aircraft accident occurs during landing, when mechanical failures, such as a malfunctioned landing gear, cause serious damage to the aircraft. Although deaths are seldom reported in such incidents, they can cause significant disruptions. In recent years, Boeing aircraft have been the subject of media attention due to several such incidents. For example, a Boeing 737-800 experienced landing gear failure at Gazipaşa Airport in Turkey, while a cargo plane operated by the U.S. Postal Service encountered a similar issue in Istanbul. In another instance, an aircraft with 73 passengers skidded off the runway after its wing caught fire at Dakar Airport in Senegal.

The most dreaded accidents, however, are those that occur mid-air, after the aircraft has taken off. Investigations into air accidents have often revealed a complex web of contributing factors, underscoring the unpredictability of such events. No airline ever intends or anticipates an accident, yet the consequences of one can be devastating. A severe crash could ground a company's operations temporarily or, in the worst cases, permanently—especially if negligence, oversight, or cost-cutting measures are found to be the cause. Failure to adhere to International Civil Aviation Organisation (ICAO) regulations or the Ministry of Aviation's guidelines could lead to ruin for an airline.

Sometimes, ground accidents can also affect aircraft already in the air. In such cases, descending planes might be forced to circle in a holding pattern while airport crews clear the runway or divert to another airport altogether. Aircraft, being complex mechanical and technological creations, require constant, rigorous inspections by licensed engineers and maintenance crews. The aircraft manufacturer's conditions of the License of Intent (LOI) mandate these checks, and failure to perform them properly can be disastrous, as post-accident investigations often reveal.

Yet, despite the best precautions, some accidents are simply unavoidable. Nature, for instance, can play a role—such as when a flock of birds crosses paths with an aircraft in flight, causing a collision as pilots struggle to avoid them. Several accidents have been attributed to such uncontrollable circumstances, illustrating the inherent risks of flying.

In this book, we will delve deeper into the myriad factors that contribute to aircraft accidents, especially those that occur in the air, and explore their causes and consequences.

1. **Weather:** This accident occurred in 1931 when an Australian National Airways Avro 618, the aircraft disappeared in severe weather while in the air from Sydney to Melbourne.
2. **Pilot Error:** In 1988, an AVir flight 3378, a Swearingen Metroline111 crashed on take-off from Raleigh to Durham airport due to the pilot error.
3. **Hijacking:** In 1988, Kuwait Airways flight 422 was hijacked enroot from Bangkok to Kuwait by Lebanese terrorists.
4. **High Speed:** In 1988 a Trans-Brazil flight cracked on a high-speed approach into Sao Paulo Guaneulhos Internal Airport.
5. **Explosive decompressor:** In 1988, Aloha airline flight in 1988, Aloha airline flight suffered an explosive decompressor during flight.

Throughout the history of aviation, numerous factors have contributed to aircraft accidents, particularly during critical moments like take-off, flight, and, most tragically, landing. The complexity of these incidents is difficult to comprehend, much like imagining the intricacies a pilot faces in real-time decision-making. One of the most challenging situations is runway overruns, a harrowing scenario where the aircraft overshoots the landing strip, often with devastating consequences.

In 1991, a tragic accident involving Indian Airlines Flight 257 occurred when it crashed into the hilly terrain of its route. Just a few years later, in 1996, another disaster unfolded when an Air Africa Antonov AN-32, operated by Moscow Airways, overloaded with passengers and cargo, failed to take off properly. It overran the runway and ploughed into a crowded market in Kinshasa, Republic of Congo. That same year, ADC Airlines Flight 086 crashed as the crew lost control while trying to avoid a mid-air collision during its approach to Lagos.

Amidst such calamities, Nigeria Airways stood as a symbol of national pride. Operating internationally and domestically from its inception in 1958 until its dissolution in 2003, Nigeria Airways, originally part of the West African Airways Corporation (WAAC), carried the Nigerian flag around the world for 44 years. The airline's reputation rested on the skill and expertise of its pilots, who were regarded among the finest globally. The rigorous selection, training, and promotion system within the airline ensured that only the most capable individuals rose through the ranks, from First Officer to Senior Officer, and finally to the esteemed position of Captain.

The pilots of Nigeria Airways were a special breed, known not only for their professionalism but for the sacrifices they and their families made during their extensive training. It was not just the technical knowledge they possessed but the pressure to maintain accuracy in every flight manoeuvre, knowing that lives depended on their skills. Names like Captains Tahal, Haye, Akintaju, Ibrahim, Nnachi, Atabo, Adebulu, Onyehoma, and All-well-Brown, among others, became synonymous with excellence in aviation. These men, many of whom have since passed, left an indelible mark on Nigeria and the world of aviation. Their contributions are written in gold and immortalized in the nation's history.

But successful flights are never the work of pilots alone. Flight engineers played a critical role in ensuring that every journey was safe. Figures like the late Sunmonu, known for his humility, Bankole, and many others, provided indispensable support in the cockpit, contributing to the safe operation of the aircraft. Each crew member relied on one another, and the synergy of their efforts was crucial to the flight's success.

Behind the scenes, equally vital to the success of Nigeria Airways were the ground engineers. Highly educated, licensed, and devoted, these professionals ensured the maintenance and safety of the airline's fleet. Without their expertise, no plane would have taken off safely. Men like Haruna, Ayo Lawal, Nwosisi, and Agom earned global recognition in the field of aviation engineering for their work at Nigeria Airways.

As we reflect on the 44-year history of Nigeria Airways, we cannot ignore the airline's accident record. Known by its IATA code "WT," Nigeria Airways experienced its share of tragedies. However, its legacy is not defined by these moments but by the dedication, skill, and honour of the people who served the

NIGERIA AIRWAYS ACCIDENT RECORDS

airline and their country. These men and women, both in the air and on the ground, helped shape Nigeria's aviation history, and their contributions continue to be remembered with respect and admiration.

1. On 20/11/69 in Lagos, a DC-1010 with flight No FN-ABD had an accident as the plane was approaching Ikeja International Airport the aircraft had just been sold to Nigeria Airways by British Overseas Corporation less than two months earlier. The accident and incident reports attributed the accident to aircraft malfunction.
2. On 04/08/71 in Jos, flight F27-200 with registration 5N—AAX, swerved off the runway and hit heaps of gravel at Jos airport caused by the cross-wind conditions.
3. On 22/01/73 in Kano, a Boeing 707—320C with registration No. JY—ADO skipped the runway and caught fire after one of the two gears collapsed. The aircraft was chartered from Alia Royal Jordan Airline for the annual Hajj Operation but was diverted to the Kano domestic route because of poor weather.
4. On 25/04/77 in Sokoto, an F–27 aircraft with registration No. N5—AAW had an accident at Sokoto airport as a result of overran the runway.
5. On 01/03/78 in Kano, an F–28 with registration No. 5N—ANA, had an accident at Kano airport, the airline lost all the passengers in the aircraft and an additional two people on the ground.
6. On 28/11/83 in Enugu, an F–28 with registration No. 5N—ANF crashed and burnt out.

7. On 10/01/87 in Ilorin, a DC—10—38 with registration No. 5N—ANR oversaw the runway as the aircraft was on a training flight.
8. On 15/10/88 in Port Harcourt, a Boeing 737—200 with registration No. 5N—ANW overran the runway on landing in heavy rain, the nose board and starboard collapsed.
9. On 02/ 10 89 in Lagos. A Boeing 737—200 with registration No. 5N—ANX, the nose gear collapsed after overrunning the wet runway.
10. On 11/07/91 in Jeddah, a DC 8 -61 with registration No. C—GMXQ and
11. Flight No. 2120 caught fire and crashed after take-off from King Abdul Azeez International Airport. The aircraft was a chartered aircraft from Canadair Company. It was to fly a pilgrimage back to Sokoto.
12. On 25/01/93 in Niamey Niger Republic, an A 310 -200 aircraft was hijacked and enrooted from Lagos to Abuja, the hijackers demanded the resignation of the government and demanded the flight be flown to Germany which was denied permission to land in Ndjamena and diverted to Niamey airport for refuelling. The aircraft was stormed by the Nigerian commandoes. Four days later, the co-pilot of the aircraft was killed.
13. On 19/12/94 in Kiri-Kasama in Jigawa State, a Boeing 707—320C with registration No. 5N—ABK and flight No. 9805 crashed after smoke emerged from the cockpit, it was reported to the pilot which diverted the attention of the pilots. The flight service was between Jeddah and Kano.
14. On 21/12/94 in Kadijah, a Boeing 707 with registration No.

5N—ABK crashed near Kadijah on a freight flight from Jeddah.

15. On 13/11/95 in Kaduna, a Boeing 737—200 with flight No. 257, and registration No. 5N—AUA experienced a wing strike on the flight following a long tailwind landing at Kaduna airport.

In May 2024, it was reported in international newspapers that three Boeing planes had a succession of accidents in three countries within a spade of two days. The first accident was reported to have occurred to a Boeing 737 -800 aircraft when its landing gear failed as it landed at Gazlpasa airport in Turkey. The second accident was a cargo plane owned and operated by a Postal System in America. It was reported to have suffered faith as it happened to the first accident that is the failure of landing gear in Istanbul. The third plane was carrying 73 passengers when it skipped off the runway after its wing burst into flames at Dakar Airport in Senegal.

From the above, it became inevitable that aircraft will have accidents, but economic loss can be minimised by regular aircraft servicing, regular training of pilots and improved navigation systems installed by the manufacturers of the aircraft. Accidents cannot be totally or permanently avoided in the air travel. Only the frequencies and fatalities in terms of lost lives in the accidents could give the airline operators and country a panicking fear of the air travellers.

Since the liquidation of the national airline, most of the senior pilots who are old in the profession have turned into businessmen while the younger ones have looked and secured employment with privately owned airlines looking for pasture fields to make two ends meet. That is life, when one door closes, another way will open.

The nation needs to remember in prayers for those who lost their lives in air crashes in respect of the airline including those of the military and private sector. May God console their families and give them the fortitude to bear the irreplaceable loss.

CHAPTER TWENTY-FIVE

THE VIRTUES OF NATIONAL INTEGRITY

INTEGRITY, AS A concept, has long held a clear and unwavering definition in the pages of any dictionary you might consult. Yet, when applied to the complexities of real-life situations, the meaning of integrity can shift depending on the individual and their motivations. While universally, it is understood to involve honesty and doing what is right, how one interprets or uses this principle can vary greatly. Some may view integrity through the lens of family values, religious beliefs, or even the understanding that actions have consequences, as embodied in the adage, "What goes up must come down" or "You reap what you sow." This notion is echoed in the wisdom of the Yoruba people and religious teachings in both the Bible and the Quran.

A vivid illustration of integrity—or the lack thereof—can be seen in the world of work and authority. Human Resources seminars often present case studies where workers, when placed under the supervision of the same individual, display different behaviours depending on the person's role. As a subordinate, a person may act with humility, but as a supervisor, the same individual may wield power differently, forgetting the saying, "Be kind to those you meet on your way up, for you may meet them on your way down." This serves as a reminder that nothing, not even life, lasts forever. As it begins, so too does it end.

For anyone seeking to understand life's fleeting nature, a visit to a hospital offers a sobering perspective. In the wards, young people battle the grip of addiction, middle-aged individuals struggle with life's limitations, and the elderly—once vibrant figures in society—now lie in beds, dependent on others for care. These were once the faces splashed across newspapers and magazines, now reduced to silence, their bodies turned from side to side for comfort. It is, at this point, one realizes how inevitable change is, and how life, in all its glory, eventually fades.

Yet many fail to grasp this. Even as individuals make decisions that affect millions, some act out of selfishness rather than considering the greater good. The mindset of "I before others" prevails in people's pursuit of power and ambition. In their desperation to reach certain positions, individuals might resort to bribery, deceit, or unholy means, visiting spiritual centres and engaging in rituals to secure their desired status. But once they ascend to power, they quickly forget the promises they made, betraying the very people they vowed to serve. History is rife with examples of such betrayal, where ambition leads to a loss of integrity. One needs only recall the political crisis in Ivory Coast, where two presidents were sworn in simultaneously. Laurent Gbagbo's refusal to accept defeat in the rerun elections marked a striking loss of integrity in the eyes of the world.

THE VIRTUES OF NATIONAL INTEGRITY

Ultimately, every human action is guided by something—whether it is a moral compass, societal expectations, or personal desires. However, how one views their actions can differ greatly from how others perceive them. Some may twist their intentions to justify decisions, arguing that their actions were right at the time. Philosophically, what may seem like the right choice in one moment may not hold in another. Nonetheless, striving for a universal standard of integrity—a life rooted in doing what is right—remains a timeless and worthy pursuit.

1. Anybody holding a public position must be able to ask himself/herself, am I the same? No matter who I am, what I have achieved is not by my might but by the grace of God. The single question that was non-African may burgle the mind of the people could be "Am I prepared to vacate my position for someone else to do better if I am no longer desired by the electorate in case of electoral position?
2. Another area of intriguing question is, "Am I willing to make decisions that are best for others even though another choice would benefit me more? This brings into focus the issue of national interest when the Late John F. Kennedy, the onetime president of the United States of America once said "Don't wait for what your country can do for you, but what you can do for your country". You don't seek political position with extreme desperation or in Nigeria terms do or die or if I can't have it, I will destroy it.
3. We have read in the newspapers, on television and at public rallies how political manifestoes were written very glossarial

without an element of implementing when and if they secure the votes of the people, realising that achievement is not a singular effort but a joint one with others who need to be persuaded to buy their ideas and support them. The question of "Can I be counted on to keep the commitments I have made to God, to myself and to the people who shall be directly or indirectly affected by my decision or policy?

4. Sometimes in life, you may need to ask certain questions probing your performance in whatever public position you find yourself, "Do I do the right thing even when no one is looking or washing me or auditing my work?". But always have it behind your mind that somebody very invisible to you and others should be looking at you. If your answer to the question of "Do I do the right thing?" is either 'no' or sometimes or hmmm, not so sure", in short anything other than capital and emphatic "YES" from the bottom of your heart and putting the picture of your God who created you and always in front of you, then you need to ask God to help you get your integrity act back together and on course.

Posterity gives everybody a second chance to change what they might have done wrong in the past either deliberately or unintentionally. You may own or pastor the largest Church or auditorium in the entire continent of Africa, you may own a business venture that is spread around the globe, you may be the Chief Imam of the most popular and admired Mosque in Saudi Arabia, sponsor and finance people to perform the Hajj pilgrimage, what you preach in your sermon must be what you practise in your daily activities.

They said people see the external look of the people but the Lord sees the inside of man. Generally, we have noted that some people take special joy when they see other people suffering which does not make us our brother's keeper. Why should the government close down an agency of theirs in which they have 100 per cent to administer without making provision for the livelihood of the people who worked there and be able to look after their families who would be affected by their simple pronouncement or signature? Why was the Nigeria Railway not liquidated and the workers who have served the company for more than forty-five years sent home without alternative means to maintain their family be made destitute? There is a friend in my area who was a railway staff and had served the mandatory maximum years of service of thirty—five years by the time the corporation was forced into liquidation. He was forced to move into a house he was putting up without doors, electricity and the ceiling was not done. He had to move away from where he rented because he could not afford the rent payment of the flat, he had rented for over 20 years when next the rent payment was due for payment. How do you want him to feel when he sees the Senators and members of the House of Representatives who are bragging and fussy because of the lecture of facts and figures extracted from the budget made available to the Central Bank of Nigeria? How do you want a man in my friend's shoes in such a situation to react if he is made to understand that a senator who served his father's land for four years would receive a pension for the rest of his life? If such a person learnt that electricity is perpetual in Niger Republic and Ghana, why should he not be concerned that fraud was the bane of our problem for lack of electricity, pipe borne water, boreholes, porthole roads that made some traders stagnant in some roads for months and lost their good in transit, unequipped hospitals and lack of security as every politician vowed to change the system when they were seeking our votes?

The last time workers of the defunct Nigeria Airways were asked to show their faces before they could be paid minor of what they could have enjoyed in the past if they received monthly pension as applied to the retiree of the NAA and FCAA, the condition some of the people were deserve some narration for public consumption and future records. Some former workers were wheeled to the assembly in wheelbarrows to show the extent of the poverty that has affected their lives. I could see some usually healthy, robust and playful during the working years who clung to the back of their sons or daughters. They became so emaciated to the extent that have departed but because they were still breathing, they could not be passed for dead and buried. Under such very serious financial agony, that they could not even afford to hire a taxi to drop them at the catering for the verification exercise. What could they make the family of people in that situation say they were proud to be Nigerians? What could they point out that could give them the grounds to make their family worth living after their breadwinner was desolated after using his youthful years to serve his fatherland?

The Ministry of Information and Communication as it is now called may use its portfolio to tell the people of Nigeria what success its tenure in office has done for the nation in the capital, but those reports have nothing to do with the lives of those who lived in the core areas of remote towns where the majority of the people I am referring to here are now congregated.

CHAPTER TWENTY-SIX

STAFF SOCIAL ACTIVITIES AT SPORTS CLUB

YOU KNOW WHAT they say, "All work and no play make Jack a dull boy." Well, Nigeria Airways had its take on that. They figured, hey, people need to let loose sometimes. So, they gave the green light to set up the Sky Power Social Club, but it was not right smack in the middle of their business space. No, they found a cosy spot for it over in Ikeja's Government Reservation Area (GRA), right by their properties division.

Now, just because you worked for Nigeria Airways did not mean you automatically got a key to the club. Nope, there was a process for that. You had to fill out a form, send it off to the finance folks, and from there, a little chunk of your paycheque got skimmed off each month to keep the club running smoothly. That covered everything—from the staff working there during open hours to the bills.

But here is the thing—nobody handed over their dues in cash. It all came out in the wash, automatically. And yeah, rules are rules, but there were exceptions. The club let in some fancy folks

STAFF SOCIAL ACTIVITIES AT SPORTS CLUB

who were not airline staff but had something valuable to offer, maybe a business connection or a professional edge. Plus, they had ties with other clubs like Ikeja Country Club, so some mixing and mingling was happening.

Most big companies, private or public, had a place for their people to kick back. I have been to the Nigerian Insurance Corporation's club, and let me tell you, it was all about leaving work at work. People could unwind and forget about the office for a while.

Some places, though, get all fancy with their social clubs. They split folks up by rank, like in the military where you have the junior staff with their hangout and the officers with theirs, called the MESS. But at Sky Power Club? Everyone was on the same playing field. No "VIP" areas or anything like that. The managing director might swing by now and then to give a pep talk, but everyone had equal say and privileges.

The club was not just a place to sip a drink—it was like a workers' parliament. People could air their grievances or get advice from a colleague on any issue, work-related or not. If you had a problem, someone was always there to lend a hand or offer suggestions. It was all about being your brother's keeper.

Naturally, cliques formed—some by department, some by interests. The engineering crew? They were tight-knit and had the cash to throw around, thanks to their extra travel allowances, which sometimes came in foreign currency. These guys were admired by many, not envied, because they worked hard for those perks. And when they passed their exams to get licensed on bigger planes, they climbed the ranks fast—no small feat!

Now, the pilots? They were a different story. They mostly stuck to themselves and did not mingle much with the other workers. The senior pilots, especially the captains, had their social scene over at the golf club behind Sky Power, rubbing shoulders with military bigwigs and top government officials. They were not exactly the friendliest bunch—rarely did they bother to wave or say hello when passing by.

Sky Power was like its own little world. Every year, the club held elections, and boy, did things get lively. Everyone wanted to know what the candidates had in mind to fix up the club or take it to the next level. The chairman's post was a big deal, mostly because that person had to work closely with the airline's top brass. And sure, anyone could run for chairman, but if you were not a department director, people would not take you too seriously.

But let me tell you about a man named Ade Ogede. Now, he never made it to chairman, but as vice-chairman, he left his mark. Ade was one of the first to get sent to Israel by the government in the '60s for aircraft maintenance training, so the man knew his stuff. He was not afraid to go toe-to-toe with management when the club needed something.

At one point, when the club hit a financial rough patch, it was Ogede who took the reins as Sole Administrator, running the show with his own money. He had a habit of keeping everyone in the loop—he would announce which beers were available or if a certain drink was hard to come by. People either loved him or loathed him, but he did not care. He did his thing and kept the club afloat when it was on shaky ground.

Ogede served as vice-chairman under multiple chairmen, and

while he never snagged the top spot, his contribution to the club's history is undeniable. The story of Sky Power Social Club would not be complete without giving him his due.

The club's history is marked by memorable elections, shaped by vibrant personalities and dramatic events. Among the notable chairmen was Mr. Epelle, who held the role while serving as Director of Marketing. I had the privilege of working under him as the General Secretary of the club. Mr. Effiong, also from the marketing department, contested for the same position but was defeated. The election, however, was marred by accusations of irregularities in a later session, evidence of malpractices led the executives to vote for the suspension of the chairman and his vice, Ade Ogede. Those who were deeply involved in that campaign and witnessed the ensuing scandals will never forget the year.

Election time was always the most exciting period in the club's history. From the close of office at 4 p.m. to the stroke of midnight, the club came alive with activity. Epelle of marketing, along with Ojokojo and Agom from engineering, left an indelible mark on the club during those times. Mr Epelle had previously been the Airline Operations Manager in the United Kingdom, overseeing operations in Europe and the United States. This background granted him a certain flair and confidence. He was sociable, approachable, and generous, creating an atmosphere where everyone around him felt important. Running against him was Mr Effiong, a controller from the same department and Epelle's deputy before being appointed special adviser to the Managing Director. Both men were from the same state, so issues of tribalism never entered the contest. Both were also strong-willed and authoritarian, unwilling to step down for one another.

The campaign between Epelle and Effiong was legendary. It was the most intense and extravagant in the club's history. Both candidates invited live bands to entertain members, encouraging them to dance away from their office stresses, with drinks flowing freely at the expense of the competitors. A debate day was set, where the candidates would outline their visions and respond to questions from members. However, just two days before the debate, Mr. Epelle was involved in a serious car accident. It was assumed he would be unable to attend, and Mr. Effiong, anticipating an uncontested victory, prepared to deliver the sole speech of the night.

To everyone's astonishment, on the night of the debate, as Mr. Effiong prepared to speak, Mr. Epelle made a dramatic entrance. He had been granted permission by his medical team to attend, and his appearance, like a ghost emerging from the mist, silenced the hall. The crowd was initially in disbelief, but when he greeted everyone with a simple "Hello," the room erupted into chaos, filled with excitement and jubilation. His presence swayed the hearts of many, even those who had not initially supported him. He won the election, though he remained in the hospital for several months afterwards.

Another notable election pitted Mr. Ojokojo, the Director of Maintenance and Engineering, against Mr. Akinde, a personnel manager in Human Resources. Mr. Akinde, though popular within his department, did not have widespread support, as many of the personnel staff were not active members of the club. They were often referred to, somewhat derogatorily, as the "church rats" of the airline—earning modest salaries and lacking opportunities to travel abroad on official duties, unlike their peers in other departments.

During a discussion among a select group of club members, the topic of the upcoming election came up. I openly questioned Mr Akinde about why he had not run as deputy to Ojokojo, as I believed it would have been a winning strategy. I doubted Akinde's ability to defeat Ojokojo, both in terms of financial backing and influence. I also argued that Ojokojo's frequent absences due to official duties would allow Akinde to deputize regularly, giving him ample leadership experience. My comments sparked a heated debate, with some opposing my views and even Mr Akinde himself expressing frustration. I stood firm in my belief that Akinde's chairmanship would not benefit the club's development projects, as he lacked the connections needed to secure funding from the airline's management.

The campaign was intense, and on the day of the election, I cast my vote and left the hall, wary of potential backlash for my outspoken position. When I returned, the results were just being announced. I ran into Mr. Akinde at the entrance, and he informed me of his defeat. I congratulated him and offered my support for his future endeavours. This, to me, was an example of political maturity—transparency and politics without bitterness.

During the tenures of Epelle and Ojoko, the club flourished, becoming a beloved social hub within the community. Its popularity soared to such heights that social bookings for the front field often exceeded capacity. True to his word, Ojoko made significant strides in improving the club's infrastructure, overseeing the expansion of buildings and the addition of a grand hall. Numerous renovations transformed the space into a vibrant venue.

Every Saturday, and occasionally on Sundays, the front open area buzzed with life, hosting grand society events such as weddings, burials, and naming ceremonies. It became a stage for renowned artists like Ebenezer Obey, Orlando Owoh, Shina Peters, and many others, who regularly graced the club with their performances. These events not only delighted attendees but also generated substantial revenue that supported the club's maintenance.

Fast forward to 2019, when I visited the site to witness the changes that had unfolded. To my shock, I discovered that the club's buildings and the front field had been sold or acquired by the nearby Bishop Virnie Cathedral Church. This once-thriving property had been transformed into an event centre, where celebrants now paid a staggering sum of 2.5 million Naira for a single day of celebration. The echoes of laughter and music that once filled the air were replaced by a different kind of hustle, marking a poignant shift in the club's legacy.

CHAPTER TWENTY-SEVEN

ISSUES OF CERTIFICATE VERIFICATIONS AND GHOST WORKERS

DURING MY SIXTEEN years in the Human Resources department at Nigeria Airways, I witnessed the repetitive enforcement of two policies that we, as employees, followed religiously each year without yielding any meaningful results. These policies, which came as directives from higher authorities, involved the annual certificate verification of staff and the hunt for ghost workers on the airline's payroll. The certificate verification process required employees to present their original certificates for comparison with those submitted during hiring. Even when staff members produced court affidavits or other legal documents to explain the absence of their originals, we were mandated to treat them as suspects, sometimes leading to suspensions or even terminations. The second exercise—the ghost worker hunt—was intended to eliminate fraudulent names from the payroll and reduce the company's wage bill. Despite the grand intentions, these efforts rarely uncovered anything significant, but we persisted year after year, as the exercise became an implied part of our duties.

This spectacle of ghost worker eliminations, especially in public organisations like Nigeria Airways, was often sensationalized by the national media. Government establishments like ours were singled out for negative attention, while other parastatals, such as the Nigeria Ports Authority or the Central Bank of Nigeria, escaped such intense scrutiny. It seemed these larger, wealthier organisations either had the means to absorb such losses or operated with a level of secrecy that shielded them from the same public outcry. Meanwhile, Nigeria Airways remained under constant watch, with every flight delay or administrative error magnified in the press. The bigger issue of fraud through ghost workers, though endemic across the nation, was swept under the rug for more privileged establishments. The fraudulent syndicate involved in inserting ghost workers into payrolls, deeply embedded in multiple departments, often operated with the complicity of both junior and senior staff, making it nearly impossible to eradicate. The cycle of loss, estimated in billions of Naira, continued, while funds that could have improved public infrastructure, security, or education flowed into corrupt pockets unchecked.

In a startling revelation, a recent news publication reported that the name of a six-year-old child had been discovered on the payroll of a government establishment. This piece of news, though sensational, left the public with more questions than answers. Key details were conspicuously missing, such as how long the child's name had appeared on the payroll, how much money had been deposited into the account, and who was responsible for collecting or withdrawing the funds. Was it the child's parents? Did they work within the organisation? Or, even more bizarrely, was this

ISSUES OF CERTIFICATE VERIFICATIONS AND GHOST WORKERS

six-year-old acting as a special adviser to the State governor? What grade level had been assigned to the child, and what allowances, if any, were being paid? These pressing questions begged for immediate answers, not just to resolve this particular case, but to prevent similar instances from occurring in other states.

In 2011, Nigeria faced the widespread issue of "ghost workers", non-existent employees who continued to draw salaries for extended periods, often unnoticed until the truth was revealed. The situation surrounding the six-year-old child on the payroll highlighted the flaws in Nigeria's system. How was the money withdrawn, by whom, and at what time of day? Certainly, a child could not walk into a bank to cash a cheque. This incident demonstrated that the nation's technology infrastructure was not yet equipped to detect such fraud, and the investigative capabilities were far below international standards. It was clear that multiple individuals inside the organisation were involved in this scheme, and they needed to be identified and brought to justice.

Why do many people still cling to reading newspapers daily? It is because they offer more than just surface-level headlines; they delve into the intricate details that television or radio broadcasts, constrained by time and advertising revenue, often overlook. Recently, some Nigerian national newspapers reported the sacking of top bank directors after it was discovered that their Master's degrees—used to secure promotions—were obtained through mere five-day online courses from U.S.-based universities. This revelation raised concerns about the hiring practices in Nigerian institutions. Before being promoted, should not the authenticity of such qualifications have been thoroughly investigated? It suggested a deeper issue, either political influence or powerful connections enabling individuals to bypass due diligence.

This is emblematic of a larger problem in Nigeria—our failure to act proactively. Instead of conducting necessary investigations beforehand, we often scramble to address issues only after they have spiralled out of control. This reactive approach also pervades the political arena. Numerous election candidates, after being declared winners by the Independent National Electoral Commission (INEC), have had their victories overturned in court due to discrepancies in their qualifications. In one notable case, a governor's win was annulled just days before his swearing-in because his deputy's certificate was found to be fake. Such incidents underscore the urgent need for a robust, well-equipped investigative system that can prevent fraud and corruption before it reaches the courts.

Recently, it was revealed that the Nigerian Senate approved a 300% salary increase for judges—an overdue move given that their pay had not been reviewed in 17 years. This revelation sparked outrage, prompting questions about what previous Chief Justices and Ministers of Justice had done to address the issue during their tenures. In contrast, a few states had taken proactive measures to ensure the welfare of their judges, offering a glimpse of what could be possible if the nation's institutions operated with foresight rather than constantly playing catch-up.

WHAT A NATION ARE WE SERVING?

CHAPTER TWENTY-EIGHT

WHO OWNS THE GRA IKEJA?

THE FIRST TIME I heard that a place was called a Government Reservation Area was when I came to Lagos in 1963 from my village in Ijebu. I was petrified and wondered how could the government own a specified area of land when what I was used to was free sales of land by the so-called landowners or landgrabbers who sold lands to free buyers on payment so that the buyers could build houses of their designed desires on such land. In so many places I have lived and travelled to in Lagos, houses were built to obscure the roads, houses were built leaving no space for drainage and without essential facilities of bathroom and toilet. I remember when I paid a visit to one of my friends at Elegbata areas in Lagos Island in 1964, the room he was occupying had an opened concreted drainage system that passed through the middle of the room where bathroom water was passing through the room to the outside gutter. Anyway, I come from a small town in Western Nigeria as it was known then where the bathroom and toilet were detached kiosks behind the house.

My curiosity about what a GRA, a humanly created, established, organised and manned by the colonial masters would look like made me sceptical and beyond imagination. I have since travelled by public transport through the GRA Ikeja and made a walk around the area and was marvelled by the layout of the place, the gap between one building and the next one, the extra land that surrounds the buildings, both in the front, at the back and sideways was unusual and I could not compare the layouts and the building structures with those at my areas of resident at Ebute Metta and Yaba, where buildings were crowdedly constructed without meaningful space and congestion of the houses, was the pattern of life I was used to.

Let me take readers back to my first visit to the areas of Lagos state in Ikeja Local Government called the Government Reservation Area commonly called (GRA) situated at Ikeja. What is GRA? GRA stands for Government Reservation Areas, therefore it was specifically carved out, located and planned to make it special and probably for a special purpose. The purpose of the Federal Government of Nigeria when the area was specially created, reserved, designed, planned and executed in terms of both road construction, drainage and house erection. Until the late 1980s when Late Lateef Jakande became the governor of Lagos State, the place was never intended and planned for the accommodation of the masses of the people of the state to live in the area. There was a big gap both in the types of houses built between those in GRA Ikeja and those in places developed by the Lagos State government building in the rural areas to relieve the ordinary people of their housing shortage. Those houses in GRA Ikeja were planned and built for the expatriates who were coming to Nigeria for employment as British Colonial Admonitors 'or as Directors in International companies. The ideology and the government of the time intended to provide these specialised employees with something similar or close to the lifestyle they were used to in their country of origin.

Therefore, it was necessary to take my audience or the readers to the time we were not lecturing or giving a speech but telling people the background history of a specialised place, therefore they were our readers and should have an open mind rather than jumping to unnecessary conclusions. Let us fly them aerially through the area called GRA Ikeja. We could start the narration from Maryland along the present Mobolaji Bank Anthony Way up to the end of Lagos State General Hospital Ikeja. It was also bounded at another end by Agege Motor Road up to Oshodi. The land owners have encroached into the original land plan and sold some edges of the federally acquired land to powerful people who could put up challenges to the Federal government's claims of ownership. Therefore, it was narrower than it was anticipated by factors of providing essential services to the people the government intend to accommodate in the areas as residents. The same scenario could be noted at the Murtala Muhammed International Airport Ikeja. The so-called land sellers have resold a reasonable proportion of the acquired airport land to people and houses were consequently built on them thereby reducing the available place to be too small to develop the airport in emulation of airports like Amsterdam and London Heathrow,

The roads constructed at GRA may not be special in terms of wideness as it was not meant to be a double carriageway. But the solidity of the roads was unusually very straight from one end to the other end merely broken by junctions and roundabouts. The fact that it was not only tarred but tarred to a high standard showed close supervision and was done by highly rated engineers on behalf of the Federal Government. I did not say there were no competent engineers employed by the Federal Ministry of Works and Housing at that time. What I am saying is that corruption has allowed shoddy jobs to become normal order and caused disrespect for our individual, family and national respect have gone to the dogs. Indignities have overshadowed dignity and national image.

The original houses in GRA were of three types, the two-story buildings, the one-story buildings and the detached houses. Most of the detached houses were meant for people with large families, while the one-story and two stories were meant for single people or those with a wife or a partner who has not got a family. The one-story and two-story buildings were mostly two bedrooms and the longest were four flats on the ground floor. These were mostly for single persons who would require a minimum space of dwelling. Spectacularly, the houses were designed to be a certain distance from the road so that both pollution and engine noise from vehicles would not be a detriment and affect the occupants while asleep. Where else in Lagos can you find similarly designed houses like that at that time when houses were just at the border of the road? Another thing of importance was the appreciation of coolness both inside the houses and the space surrounding them. That was achieved by the plant of trees not necessarily those that would produce edible fruits e.g. mango trees, guava trees, orange trees, etc, but any trees that the branches would shed shades. Thirdly the houses were built on acres of land surrounded on both sides, in front and backyards and sideways with enough grassed land to play mini-games of whatever interest individuals.

Comfort is the British priority of living in their houses, comfort is not determined by the size of the house and their location but by the provision of all relevant and related services. Security was one of the list priority desires hence the Police College was established close-by to make sure that inhabitants of the area would have the mentality of security whether they were at home or on an assignment duty outside the country having the assurance that their family is protected. The Police Station was at a shouting distance. Shopping and shopping complexes played a double role as a place to buy what they were used to in their countries and a place to meet and see the people who lived near you and have conversations about things of common interests hence Kingsway Supermarket was located in an important and strategic roundabout that was walkable and with sufficient parking facilities to accommodate reasonable number of customers vehicles at a time. Most of the residents were imagined to be Christians by faith since they brought Christianity with trade to open us with the rest of the world and stop human sacrifice and slave trading which were the traditions we inherited from our ancestors. A Methodist Church was established for residents to worship their God on Sundays. The Church was later renamed after the first Bishop of Lagos in the name of Leslie Gordon Vining.

The Church was and still is attended by people who matter most in Lagos society such as top military Officers (retired and still serving) industrialists and successful politicians who have held key political positions in the nation. We must not forget to mention looking after the health of the people who reside in GRA. The present General Hospital Ikeja was not established in its present location by accident but started as a small health centre, it was established to meet the needs of the residents of GRA and their families. It became a full-fledged hospital gradually and was renamed General Hospital Ikeja. An Industrialist and philanthropist named Chief Mobolaji Bank Anthony showed his hands of generosity to the people of Lagos State by building and equipping the premises of a maternity ward building named in his name. The road from Maryland to the hospital was renamed Mobolaji Bank Anthony Way, though the main entrance to the hospital was situated at the beginning of Oba Akinjobi Street toward the estate. Today, the hospital has been renamed as Lagos State University Teaching Hospital

To complete a mini town within the township of Ikeja, there was Ikeja Country Club for the expatriate residents to socialise, play outdoor games and take their families out after a day of work or at the weekends. The Country Club's name was derived from the area which was created like a country. All sorts of games were made available to keep members engaged for several hours a day.

We have now reached the stage where we must disclose the original occupiers in terms of ownership of the estate as we shall call it henceforth. The GRA Ikeja was established by the Federal Government of Nigeria for the exclusive occupation of foreign workers of Nigeria Airways. Therefore, all the houses in the estate were built for all classes of foreign staff of the airline from the pilots, Engineers, Traffic Controllers, Marketing etc. Because of its closeness to the airport, they could get home late as their schedules demanded. In times of emergency, messages could be easily passed to the specialists' staff required to deal with the matter as promptly as possible.

As the nation's governing system changed from the civilian government to the military regime due to the coup de tat of 1966, law, order and procedures of the ways we do things have to jump out of the window into thin air. New tax collectors have come to the town. The military needs to be described as we all knew what we went through in their first two years in power. Whether dressed in uniform or civil dress, they did not want to pay for their transportation either by road or by train, they could drive their vehicles either military or private anyhow and anywhere with impunity. Only God could count the number of innocent drivers and pedestrians who were killed not only by accidental discharges, but once you have one of them as a friend or relative, you could do what you desire with your enemies either by the act of disappearance or beaten to a pulp so that they would give up the ghost in the hospital. If any hospital would accept them for admission and treatment anyway.

Some Nigerian Air Force (NAF) officers were legally allocated quarters at GRA Ikeja because of the closeness or proximity of the place to the airport and the fact that the hazard of their assignments could warrant them being called upon at any time for emergency duties. When I was keeping the records of the Nigeria Airways houses or quarters in GRA, several times I made representation to the airline management about the company quarters which were illegally occupied and most of them were forcefully occupied, when a staff has just vacated them on the ground of retirement or dismissal from the service of the company. As preparations were in progress to reactivate the flat for another staff to move in, information would get to us from the property division that the key to the door had been replaced and a stranger had occupied the quarters. On checking up by the security of the airline, the new occupants were always military officers either the Army, the Air Force or the Police and usually that was the end of that story. If the house is undergoing renovation for the next occupier or was there any legal dispute in court on the property, that was never anything to worry about at that stage. They always bring a carpenter to change the main entrance key to the gate and the front door and nothing and nobody could approach the place to ask questions as to how they became the new landlord of the place.

When Lagos State was created, Ikeja in its entirety became an important town. This gave the government of the State the right to all the lands under her control and it became the capital of the state. The land at GRA came under the ownership of the state and the then Governor Lateef Jakande had the vision of using any available land for a project that would give the state an enviable status in such areas that would be to the benefit of the people in schools building, health centres and sports facilities. A land behind the country club was earmarked for the construction of the Lagos State Stadium for all the games activities which was to include a Football field, athletics and whatever would be desirable and attract visitors to put the state at the forefront of sports in the world. The place was cleared and construction works were in progress but after the military takeover, we reliably learnt that about ₦6 billion Naira was already or almost expended on the project.

As we are known in Nigeria as a country of no continuity, as there was a change of government from civilian to military, Jakande was relieved of his position and a military man assumed the position of governorship in Lagos as a change of baton of governance. To show that the civilian regime was inefficient and corrupt, which was always the core of military announcements when there was a coup in the country, almost all Jakande's programmes and policies were changed and abandoned to give credibility to the change of government. All the constructions and other infrastructures carried out on the new stadium were demolished. After some time, the place was allocated to some powerful individuals who built their choices of houses on the land. I am not challenging what the government has done or failed to do, it is left for the populace to come to their independent conclusion.

Nigeria Airways had its property division at the GRA very close to the Sky Power Club and a few steps distant from Bishop Vinnie Anglican Church. There was always something to see and notice and there could be a counterclaim of the owner of the land between these two bodies. I will not venture into any argument about the ownership. Let a sleeping dog lie and soundly undisturbed. This is now a democratic regime where freedom of speech was guaranteed not by the Constitution of Nigeria as that cannot be relied upon hundred (100) per cent but guaranteed by the Human Rights Convention of the United Nations.

The property division of the airline had the Sky Power Sports Club in front of it. The land starts from Agege Motor Road to Oba Akinjobi Road which belonged to the airline but some influential people in Nigeria Society were looking for an ideal place to start a Golf Club, initially they asked Nigeria Airways management for a small portion of the land to serve as a place for their members to meet after work to socialise. As their members increased and they comprised the timbers and calibres of the society from the military to industrialists to judiciary, they became authoritative and bold to acquire all the land to expand their activities. There are so many Nigerian Airways Pilots who were members of the Golf Club by registration and they prefer going to the Golf Club to attending the Sky Power Club as they prefer to associate with their class of the people in the society. They became birds with the same feather flow in the same direction. Class division is inevitable in a society of over 225 million people. It became inevitable that Nigeria Airways management could not demand the yearly rental payment to the airline which abruptly ceased and they started claiming ownership and the airline was not willing to challenge their encroachment.

Now that the airline had been demised through liquidation, there was nobody to challenge them about the acres of land. Today the Church has turned the massive grassed land in front of the Sky Power Club into car park facilities for their members. The property division site of the airline had been taken over with a new model Event Centre where you have to pay about ₦2.5 million Naira to hire the centre for a one-day socialising of wedding, burial or birthday celebration.

CHAPTER TWENTY-NINE

FEDERAL MINISTRY OF AVIATION— A MILKING COW

SINCE THE DAWN of the current democratic era in Nigeria, the Federal Ministry of Aviation has seen a revolving door of political appointees—both male and female—most of whom were middle-aged. Yet, their collective tenure has largely left the public disillusioned, with little to celebrate in terms of their contributions to the development of the ministry. Despite the high expectations that come with the position, few of these appointees can point to any tangible improvements or lasting legacies in the agencies or parastatals under their care. Their inability to make significant progress has raised concerns about the integrity of the modern political class in Nigeria and whether they have forgotten that history will one day judge their performance. Many arrived at their offices surrounded by an entourage of security personnel and a fleet of vehicles, engaging in what seemed like ceremonial protocols. However, beneath this display of power, corruption often lurked. And in a cruel twist of fate, those who once followed them—carrying their files and ensuring their smooth passage through crowded spaces—may later be the ones investigating them. The journey from being in charge to being summoned by the DSS or facing allegations of corruption is a stark reminder of how power can quickly shift.

One needs only look at the case of the former Governor of a state who, after failing to honour an invitation from security officials, found himself cornered on the roof of his own house. Or the former Governor of the Central Bank of Nigeria, who was assured that his detention would last only a night or two but ended up spending months in custody. These incidents echo the adage, "What goes up must come down." Of all federal ministries in Nigeria, the Ministry of Aviation has, unfortunately, garnered a reputation for being one of the most corrupt. Its long history of financial misconduct and money laundering is unparalleled, raising questions about why it is seemingly more exposed than others. Perhaps, unlike other ministries, its dealings are audited more frequently, or maybe it lacks the discretion others possess to hide corruption under the carpet. Over time, corruption within the ministry appears to have been passed from one minister to the next. In a nation where dishonesty has become an accepted norm, those who know how to tell the right stories and align themselves with the ruling political party often find themselves appointed to high offices. As we examine the performance of three former Ministers of Aviation, it becomes clear that their legacies are far from hidden or confidential—these are public stories widely discussed in Nigerian newspapers, on television, and across social media. Their tenure and the problems that plagued them serve as cautionary tales in the annals of Nigerian politics.

1. Mrs. Stella Oduah Ogiemwonyi is always called Oduah
2. Mr. Femi Fani- Kayode
3. Mr. Hadi Sirika

Stella Oduah

Stella Oduah, as she was regularly referred to in the media, was the first lady to be appointed as the Minister of Aviation since the present democratic dispensation. She was a Senator before being appointed as the Minister between the period of 04/07/2011 and 12/02/2014. She was a Minister for three years only. She did not resign her appointment which could have made it honourable. She was relieved of her duties due to numerous corruption allegations coming to the ears and the table of the president then. The Punch Newspaper was one of the national newspapers that reported and published an article which showed that she had four companies and the accounts of these companies were frozen by the government anti-corruption agency for alleged indebtedness of the following amounts:

1. $16,412,819.06 and another ₦100,493,225.59 as tendered in a piece of documentary evidence at the High Court in Lagos. She was reported to have registered the four companies in her name. The companies referred to are as follows:

    (a) Sea Petroleum and Gas Company Limited.
    (b) Sea Shipping Agency Limited
    (c) Rotary Engineering Service Limited
    (d) Tour Afrique Company Limited

These companies had twenty-one bank accounts which she operates. According to the publication, she has been involved in numerous controversies. Among those controversies when she was the minister of aviation was the allegation of highly inflated purchase of BMW bulletproof cars for the ministry without following the laid down process or due process. The bullet-proof cars were purchased for her office use and indirectly she would be the user of the vehicles. The National Assembly: Senatorial and the House of Representatives at the 9th session have bought SUV bulletproof cars for themselves. When asked why they decided to buy such expensive cars at a time when the economy of the country was stumbling, one of them whose statement can be taken as representing the lot of them said because the roads in Nigeria are very bad and the security of the country is also bad, hence, members need to be protected.

2. She was said to have lied about her educational qualifications. She claimed to have obtained a degree in Master of Business Administration (MBA) at the time as the University did not even have a graduate school not to mention a postgraduate programme. The Economic and Financial Crime Commission (EFCC) indicted Stella Oduah and the Nigerian Subsidiary of a Chinese construction company called CCECC in an alleged fraudulent cash transaction of ₦5 billion over five months in 2014. As it is embedded in our country Nigeria, no court has found her guilty of any offence.

3. She contested for a political position in the Senate and was declared in her constituency to have won the election but on appeal of one of the co-contestants for the result to be

re-examined, the court disqualified her and removed her from the Senate. I am optimistic that that will not be the end of her political struggles.

Femi Fani—Kayode:

He was the Minister of Aviation from 07/11/2006 and 29/05/2007, which means he covered the covet position for six months. He was arrested by the EFCC in July 2008 in connection with the alleged misappropriation of a ₦19.05 billion "Aviation Intervention Fund". The investigation found no evidence of corruption against him. You need to be smart and sweet-mouthed to be a politician in Nigeria. When some class of people including officials say something is pure white, tell them to look at it the second and third times before they can be sure of what they were speaking about. Tell them it is the opposite colour, tell them and be insistent on it and if you are a Godfather or a person of heavy purse to throw dollars about, you will be vindicated.

The Senate Committee on Aviation in early 2008 recommended that Femi Kani-Kayode be banned from holding public office for five years but withdrew the request as he had been found not guilty of any crime by the court hence has not violated the law of the land. His arrest in 2008 was as a result of a charges on 47 counts of money laundering. In his self- defence, he stated that he was innocent and that the monies that was found in his accounts were funds received from his own private businesses and were legitimate sources and had nothing to do with government funds. He said that the investigation of President Yar-Adua government and the one of the EFCC were politically motivated and he was prosecuted the same way as other colleagues who are ardent supporters of President Obasanjo government. He mentioned people like El-Rufai, one- time Minister of Federal Capital Territory (FCT), and Nuru Ribadu who was the chairman of the EFCC when it was first established as examples for their ties to President Obasanjo when he was on the thrown of power.

Femi Fani-Kayode was discharged and acquitted on 01/072008 by a Federal High Court sitting in Lagos on the two count charges of money laundering preferred against him by the EFCC. The court held that the EFCC was unable to prove their charges beyond reasonable doubt and consequently acquitted him on the charges against him. The issue of collaborating with some foreign contractors when he was the minister who awarded the contract for the runway contract to raise the quotations for contracts by topping it with certain percentage which would be his own portion were never mentioned nor debated in the court procedures. He is well known as a smart guy in all ramifications up to his marital history and political activism. His political records show he jumps from one political party to another political party and one of the motives was stated to be relevant and avoid prosecutions. He often choses to be a spokesman for a political party whether he was elected or he chooses himself for the political party. Some people who did not like him often called him Political prostitute.

FEDERAL MINISTRY OF AVIATION—A MILKING COW

Hadi Sirika

Hadi Sirika is from Katsina State hence he won his first election to the Federal House of Representative in 2007. In 2011, he won another election this time to the House of Senate. When he was in the Federal House of Representative, he was selected as Portal Vice Chairman of the Millenium Development Goal (MDG). Less I forget, he was a commercial Pilot by profession. He was selected as a member of Senate committee on Aviation and was later appointed as the Minister of State for Aviation under the Federal Minister of Transportation until the expiration of President Buhari regime in 2023. He attended Petroleum Helicopter Institute in the USA as training pilot. He also attended Flight Safety International and Delta Aeronautic also in USA, He was a licenced pilot. According to the record available on Hadi Sirika, he was appointed as Minister of Aviation from 2019 and 2023.

He wanted to stamp his name in gold on the Aviation history of Nigeria by re-introducing the Nigeria Air as a national career for the country. But history will never overlook the ways he approached the laudable project. Something all the Nigerians were yearning for a long time. His approach was seen as economic and social failure when compared with the South Africa airline, Ethiopian Airlines lifting passengers from Nigeria because Nigeria lacked a national career of their own. He went to paint one of the Ethiopian aircraft with a logo of Nigeria Air and brought it to Abuja for launching by the President of Nigeria to attend such a shambolic and deceitful inauguration unaware of the chains of events. In a country where intelligence is ripe and at work, some of the intelligent agents ought to have had a wind of knowledge of what was in the pipeline and the information should have been passed to the President and should have put a stop to such a scam.

It was reported by one of the newspapers that the EFCC had frozen an account belonging to Abubakar Ahmed Sirika, the biological brother of the immediate past minister of aviation Hadi Sirika over an alleged ₦8.06 billion contract fraud in the Federal Ministry of Aviation. The Nation newspaper, one of the most credible newspapers in Nigeria which can be trusted and relied upon for whatever it reported said, that the anti-graft agency after the arrest of Abubakar Sirika over contract fraud worth about ₦3.2 billion that was traced to his private company known as Enrigios Nigeria Limited. Records showed that Abubakar Sirika was a Civil Servant and a grade level 16 Officer which made him a Deputy Director at water resources in Abuja. We are made to understand that four big contracts were awarded to Abubakar from Enigiros Nigeria Limited when his brother was in charge of the ministry. Abubakar is listed as the managing director and Chief Executive Officer of the companies and the sole signatory to the two banks the company was operating. The four contracts the ex-minister awarded to his brother which were not executed but were fully paid for in advance were as follows:

(a) Construction of the Terminal Building at Katsina Airport for the sum of ₦1.3 billion.
(b) Fire Truck Maintenance and Refurbishment Centre at Katsina.

(c) Procurement and Installation of elevators air conditioners and power generator house in Aviation House.

(d) Abuja ₦615 million procurement of Magnus Aircraft, and Simulator for Nigeria College of Aviation Technology, Zaria for the sum of ₦2.3 billion.

The investigators revealed that a payment of ₦3.2 billion out of the total contract was made to Engrios Nigeria Limited. Upon receipt of the payment, Abubakar allegedly transferred the money to different companies and individuals. The Investigators also alleged that no trace of work had been done on any of the contract items mentioned above to date.

NIGERIA AIR

The Nation Newspaper published a publication that the EFCC has summoned the immediate past minister to appear before it over the controversial Nigeria Air project which he claimed had engulfed the huge sums of ₦3 billion. Sirika is expected to appear before the anti-graft agency within the week of the invitation. Sources close to the Guardian Newspaper revealed that the commission would look at the ₦3 billion sunk into the project though some stakeholders insisted that over ₦80 billion was expended on the project. An anonymous speaker who does not want his name to be mentioned said, "I can confirm that there is an ongoing investigation in that regard."

The anti-graft agency had also questioned some officials of Nigeria Air over the recent launch of the airline in Abuja. They claimed to have already questioned some official of Nigeria Air but nothing was revealed as their disclosure. That is how to be a Nigerian. The committee was made to understand that the Nigeria Air aeroplane was garbed in Nigeria colour, and the stakeholder of the project was enraged that an Ethiopian airline that landed in Nigeria with Ethiopian Air particulars was paraded as a national career. The former Minister in self-defence at a recent ARISE TV News Channel programme as he was interviewed on the subject matter said, "The landing of the Ethiopian aircraft in Abuja was a marketing strategy.

From the extensive analysis stated by at least three ministers and their records in office, we can philosophically assume that the Federal Ministry of Aviation now renamed by President Ahmed Tinubu as Federal Ministry of Aviation and Aeronautic has ever been the most corrupt and ministered by most arrogant, shameless and worst reputations for scandal and money launderings. Mention another ministry of Federal status that has ever been probed and ridiculed in the Federation like it. From the records of birth of the minister Sirika, none of the mentioned ministers was over sixty at the time they were appointed to be ministers. These are the types of people the Nigerian populace is looking forward to leading the country in the future but alas, they made personal interests and gains over the national development and advancements and destroyed their political future and reputations. But when you have it in your mind that most Nigerian politicians have no integrity, good reputations and image, they do not think of their image you would not be surprised by the reported outcomes.

Ministers and government officials at the Ministry need to be at alert and made to understand that their behaviours and performances are monitored rigorously during their tenure. It does not make sense to summon a minister to answer or give explanations on corruption after his tenure in the office probably two years later when he might have lodged what he or she has stolen and laundered the money to various accounts to avoid concrete evidence to render the facts of the matter and allegations to become absolute impactable evidence. The huge stolen money could have been used to increase the salaries and benefit of the judiciary, train and equip technically the EFCC officials and other agencies that are established to fight crimes and corruption in our country.

On "Journalist Hangout", a programme on TVC, Babatunde Kolawole Otitoju, a renowned journalist and one of the anchors of the programme mentioned that civil servants are extremely corrupt in Nigeria and were the biggest problem facing the country in terms of revenue-generating as the government money goes into their pockets. He categorically mentioned that he was aware of some grade level 09 officers in some ministries who have estates and probably had registered companies with which they divert government contracts or used their relation names and bank accounts who are at the helm of affairs that made payments into their company accounts for contracts never executed. We have seen the case of Sidi Sirika and his biological brother narrated earlier in this chapter as a typical example and an eye-opener.

The governments at the central and state levels need to be proactive by monitoring what is going on using their intelligent gathering dragnets to be proactive and to expose official corruption instead of flogging a dead horse. Most corrupt cases in the courts never resulted in decisions that sent people to jail that could frighten future generations from following in their footsteps. Hence cases die a natural death after wasting billions of Naira on investigations and hiring Lawyers to prosecute the offenders.

NIGERIA HAS BECOME A
COUNTRY THAT CAN BARK
BUT CANNOT BITE.

CHAPTER THIRTY

LIFE OF PENSIONERS OF NIGERIA AIRWAYS

THE BIBLICAL SCRIPTURE says, "Thou shall enjoy the fruits of thy labour" (Psalm 128:2). That was the commandment of the Lord to the Christian and it as well apply to the Muslim brothers. I am convinced that the Holy Quran must have something similar to say or commandments to the followers of the Holy Prophet Mohammed (S.A.W). That commandment does not appear to be put into operation in Nigeria. With all the Churches and Mosques scattered in every corner of towns and villages, our politicians found taking their places at the front line of the Muslim Praying grounds and the Christians on the front chairs or pews of the Churches on Sundays and at the super camps, yet our leaders are just too thick skinned their attitudes is, "Preach to me and let me go" from both religions congregations which are domineering in the country. Facebook is my favourite medium of all self-entertainment because it allows much freedom of speech and display of comparable and competitive photographs.

Wherever I feel down and bored or unamused, I enjoy going through Facebook and Tick-Tocks on my mobile phone for current networking information to feed my eyes or something to laugh about. One of the two photographs of assembled people of the same objective and category was the one with the caption, "The Pensioners" but it was taken from two countries, one in the United Kingdom and the other picture was taken in Nigeria. In narration, the picture taken in the UK showed the hands of the Lord or Allah was with them and providing them with His blessings through the government of the country They looked fresh, robust, well fed, well dressed with a cup of tea in front of each of them in an environment that could only be compared to the Kingdom of God on earth. In Nigeria, such a dignified place could only probably be at an event centre where the host has paid about ₦5 million for that day get get-together. The UK picture could probably be organised by their local government Council for the pensioners in their Borough to meet and socialise to reflect on their past togetherness, or of where they have worked or one of them was celebrating a low-key birthday with the supply of menu- menus.

The Nigeria picture showed people of common interest who gathered together to agitate for their rights which has been denied them for many years. There was nothing to write home about their outlooks. Their mode of dress looked like somebody who had not been washed for two years or more. The dresses they put on looked like they had been owned by somebody else for over twenty years. Most of them were wearing bathroom slippers and they carried small files which must have contained their documentation.

Looking at them critically without exaggerations showed that they were full of worries, anxiety, traumatised, confused and uncertain about their future. Hunger has taken a greater proportion of their bodies and hope was not in their dictionary, nor their Bible or Holy Quran.

This is the situation that made Nigeria's class of pensioners assembling become a ritual and they are often located in front of their former employers or pension offices in case of good news may be announced by the government to their former civil servants about their pension payments which has run into many years. Also, they can be seen along the roadsides as a sign of confusion about where they were to go to demand their pension payments because previous pension office locations given to them to attend, have never been officially opened to them nor any information pasted on any side of the building to inform them of the situation of things. They were dribbling like football on playing fields of matches. Frustration and hopelessness have turned both the Christians and the Muslims into one combined religious group and a congregation of prayer though separately at a place of prayers on Fridays. When there is no hope, despairs can turn a human being into what he doesn't desire. The prayer group become their last hope when their employer particularly the Federal government and the state government have left them in a limbo. They appoint a pastor within themselves to preach hope and encouragement to them. All the conditions of service on their contract of employment which stipulated their entitlements in terms of gratuities and guaranteed pension become unimplementable stories. Imagine a dedicated teacher who has served in so many schools and the government stipulated a maximum mandatory period of thirty- five years and was given an elaborate send-off by his trade union and another send-off by the staff and colleagues at the last school he had served, but the government as an employer failing to honour their pension and gratuities.

Five years later, some of the students he had taught before retirement would see him or her in a dreadful appearance looking so emancipated, haggard and improperly kept. Would such a student be impressed or be willing to follow the line of career that his predecessors followed as he would not be prayerful to suffer the same faith in the future? Gratuity is a payment, typically of money made to an employee by an employer in recognition of love and meritorious service or a special act of deed by the employee. It is an established custom in many countries to provide a gratuity to certain service employees such as waiters and taxi drivers. In an employment contract, you are guaranteed a certain percentage of money for a service period which makes the amount of money for entitlement vary as it is based on years of service and the grade level someone was at the time of exit from the establishment.

Pension on the other hand for an employment-based retirement plan is an arrangement to provide people with an income during retirement when they are no longer earning a steady income from employment. Often retirement plans require both the employer and the employee to contribute some amount of money to a fund during their employment to receive a defined benefit upon retirement. It is a tax-deferred savings vehicle that allows the tax-free accumulation of a fund for later use as retirement income. This is the characteristic you find in companies. In government establishments where you are entitled to a certain amount which is determined by the number of years you served and the grade level you attained at the time of retirement. Let it be on record that by government regulations, your retirement time may be determined by two factors. The first is your age i.e. at the age of sixty (60) years you need to bow out of service or you have put in a service of thirty—five (35) years.

NIGERIA AIRWAYS LIMITED

In the earlier years, Nigeria Airways was known for its commendable management, particularly in the timely payment of gratuities and pensions. Employees took pride in the organisation, which had earned a reputation for credibility. However, this image began to tarnish as the airline fell into a troubling pattern of yearly retrenchments, particularly at the close of each year. While employees in other organisations under the same Ministry of Aviation, such as the Federal Civil Aviation Authority (FCAA) and the Nigerian Airports Authority (NAA), were engaged in negotiations for salary increments and improved working conditions, Nigeria Airways' employees faced an entirely different reality. December, once a time of hope and celebration, turned into a month of sorrow and anxiety. Workers, uncertain of their future, were consumed by fear, not knowing if they would still be employed when January arrived.

The process by which employees were selected for retrenchment was shrouded in mystery. There was no clear set of criteria, leaving everyone vulnerable and unsure of their fate. Retrenchment, by definition, is a cost-saving measure undertaken by companies facing economic difficulties, typically when expenses—like staff salaries—exceed a certain percentage of revenue. However, at Nigeria Airways, the rationale behind the annual layoff exercises seemed arbitrary. The lack of transparency fuelled confusion and resentment among the workforce, as there were no established guidelines that could reassure employees or justify the retrenchments fairly and equitably. The standard procedures for such actions, grounded in fairness and adherence to legal frameworks, seemed to be overlooked, leaving a legacy of trauma and uncertainty in its wake.

1. **Age of the employee**: When one is 60 or close to that age, he should be prepared to leave the employment so that the young ones can climb the ladder of upgrading or leadership.
2. **The principle of last in first to go**: This means when you want to reduce your workforce, you should try to retain your experienced workers and lay off those who are viewed as new in the organisation.
3. Other criteria that should have been used to avoid being taken to court for unlawful dismissal or retirement was on the grounds of the inability of the staff to cope with modern technology in the industry.
4. Merging sections of relevance into one to reduce the number of workers by a certain percentage. This is where the principle of last in first out is applicable. But this has no basis in efficiency or performance.

Retrenchment was based on where there are thirty people in two sections of a department that need to be merged into one for economic and profitability grounds and the need to reduce the number of workers now in one section from thirty-five to maybe twenty people. This is where the controller who used to be Deputy Director may come in to select those whose job assessments justified their retention. In most cases, the controller of a section in Nigeria Airways may not have a say on who would be retained and those to be relieved of their posts in his section.

I could recollect the 1986 retrenchment where about three thousand six hundred (3600) workers were relieved of their employment en-mass, the personnel manager who was mandated to carry out the assignment never had a say either in who was to be on the list or to add or remove any name from the list. He was just obeying the commands of the management. As I stated somewhere previously in the past chapters of the book, he never attended the office during the normal working hours of the day. He and his team always came to the office in the evening times when workers had closed and left for their homes for the day to avoid the suspicion that something was in the pipeline. There was a clause in the retrenchment regulations which could have given the workers retrenched the power to challenge their retrenchment in a court of law if they were not given any reason for the action or decision of the management to send them packing. To avoid such challenges in the Law Courts or employment tribunals by former directors who were so affected, the airline looked for a clause to justify their reasons for being asked to leave the company as there were no previous records of disciplinary offences in their files. A very powerful and well-placed director was compulsorily retired and the reason given for the action was a funny and unimaginable: was "incapable of coping with the modern technology", that is for somebody who had served the airline for nearly sixty years from the boyish age and low junior level to the highest level of the echelon of the highest ladder. By the clause, he was being told that he was of no use in that capacity. There is no redress of law he can use as a case to redress his sudden and involuntary retirement except by the lawyers who just want to take his money with a promise to defend his case in the law court.

The problem of failure to pay both the gratuities and pensions emanated from that mass retrenchment of 1986. Where could the airline afford the funds to pay that number of workers just laid off? For reasons not honestly disclosed to the general public which made people have insinuation and numerous speculations about the reasons given by the government and the airline management for the liquidation of the national airline in 2003 was based on the assumptions that the workers were corrupt and overstaffed. The government said that the airline was making losses, was not efficient, the staff were corrupt and lacked enough aircraft to justify its continuous existence and operations. The irony of the matter was, that the government appointed the management director, the departmental directors and the board of directors or the Presidential Task Force as the case may require to carry out all the executive duties and orders of flights which were not commercially desirable, profitable, and not to mention of not been paid for after the services were carried out as commanded from the above.

Secondly, let us go into some instances of these types of situations, the Hajj Operation was a yearly event that Nigeria Airways carried out on behalf of the government or the other of the government as the major shareholder in the airline. This was politically taken away from the airline and given to political bigwigs who are not operating an airline but as a political compensation for their loyalties in the past and the future as a member of the political board of trustee of the political party in government. After the people who went to perform the Hajj pilgrimage, some people who are professional traders could have as many as ten to twenty bags of excess luggage left behind in Jeddah because the operator would not carry their extra luggage. The people would lobby the Presidency which would mandate the minister of aviation to ensure that Nigeria Airways was made to evacuate all the left behind pieces of luggage back to Nigeria within a specified time. On many occasions, Nigeria Airways could make as many as six to ten trips of flights in cargo planes owned and hired by the national carrier to retrieve the pieces of luggage back to Nigeria. The Federal Ministry of Aviation does not often pay for these uncontracted flights. Do we call it charity or national assignment without due compensation?

When a new managing director was announced by the government for the airline, particularly if the appointee was from one of the Armed Forces, the staff of the airline often assumed the man had nothing to add to the structure and development of the airline than to state in his annual reports to the minister of the aviation how many workers he had retrenched. It was an assumed fact that he retrenched over three thousand and six hundred employees which was the reason one of their terms of contract on the position was extended. The regulations guiding retrenchment had a clause that once one is retrenched, the person would not be taken back again into the employment of the airline. This policy was breached by a lady of influential connection and boastful lady in personnel who was retrenched and after lobbying was re-engaged in the same grade level back to the company. Heaven never falls and nobody dares raise any complaints, as if one did see nor hear, your name would be on one in the next retrenchment exercise. The place was like a prison yard or correction centre where you must behave like a zombie if you have the desire to survive.

The Controller of Audit retired in grade level 16, and he was given another contract of re-employment in grade level 15 because he was one of the caucus and cabal in the airline of special people. Does it mean there are no younger people in the division with better qualifications or somebody be deployed from another division of finance as a form of promotion or upgrading to replace him? That was political ingenuity. The government made the law and they could violate it with impunity. Only the poor are suffering because they do not have the political bigwig to fight for their courses. Who says we are equal before the Constitution of the Federal Republic of Nigeria; I can challenge that as an important lawyer like Femi Falana is doing in the courts of law. on the issue of Human Rights.

One speculation on the liquidation of the national career which had good grounds was the re-warding of the Nigeria Airways House and the Engineering and Maintenance workshop to Arik AIR. There was nothing I would like to say about it other than to let people know what people were saying about it. Did Air Arik pay any money to fund the Nigeria Airways to augment the payment of the pension of the former workers? Only the government knew that side of the history. Or did the people in power unilaterally give the places to Arik Air because of their investments in the airline? Either Christians or Muslims, let the Lord see our hearts and judge us according to the rules of laws.

Between 2003 and 2018, a period of sixteen years, no provision was arranged nor made for the airline former employees to earn pension. It was under the Presidency of Buhari that approved the sum of ₦78 billion for the pensioners to be paid. It is very sad and unimaginable for me to say that ₦33 billion of the money is yet to be released for payment. It would be very distressful if I were to write what has happened to so many former workers of the airline due to the lack of money they were entitled to and being denied, and the hazards they have gone through and still going through, they were more than what the Jews suffered when they were in captivity in Germany during the Second World War (WWII). Because some of them could not pay their rent on the place they had been luxuriously living for years, their landlords ejected them, and some had to rent a room in a face me-I face you house which made their spouses divorce or abandon the marriage. Many could no longer pay the school fees of their children; the children have abandoned schooling and joined the people at the garages as "AGBEROS". Many have died of curable illness because they could not afford to buy the medically recommended medications. Some have gone back to their village of origin out of shame and indignity when there was nowhere else to go. Some have murdered their wives unintentionally but out of depression and mental failures to cater for the family and the women were ridiculing their husbands before their family and the children.

In 2018, the workers were invited to attend a verification exercise for the payment of the pension arrears as were humanely approved for them by President Buhari. The first shock I had was that it was not the total money approved that was to be paid that year, only ₦45 billion was released. We shall mention what might have happened to the balance of ₦33 billion later in the chapter. What were the problems of pension non-payment in Nigeria generally? The most significant were the attitudes, beliefs, and inhuman civil servants who wanted to steal what they could grab today and now so that their families would not suffer as these are going through today when they retired. Let me mention some relevant episodes:

1. Abdulrasheed Maina was a senior administrator at Customs, Immigration and Prison Pension (CIPPS). He was appointed as the Chairman of the Pension Reform Task Team (PRTT) by the Federal Government from 2010 to 2013. In 2013 he was accused of fraud amounting to over ₦20 billion. He was hence dismissed by the Office of Head of Service from the position of chairmanship and was declared wanted by the EFCC after he allegedly fled to Saudi Arabia. in 2017, He was secretly reinstated into public service in the Ministry of Foreign Affairs but was fired by President Buhari who ordered him to be probed. In 2020, during his trial, he fainted in the courtroom. He was sentenced to eight years in prison. A civil servant doing that to other civil servants. Where are our religious doctrines then?

2. Ahmed Idris, was the Accountant General of the Federation of Nigeria. He was alleged to have stolen ₦109.5 billion during his tenure in the office. He was alleged to have returned $900,000 in cash to the government so that the case would not go into hearing as a settlement out of court. Some Nigerians are fast and super intelligent. He was accused of abuse of his office and compromising government platforms such as the Treasury Single Accounts (TSA).

From these two cases above, the huge sums of money allegedly stolen or laundered, we can see that the issue of pensioners payment in Nigeria not receiving their pensions did not start from the government alone but from the people who are entrusted to look after the welfare of the people already retired and the generations yet to retire in the future. When civil servants of Abdulrasheed Maina status, a civil servant who had worked in the customs with all the privileges of corruption must have committed to the organisation to manage the welfare of a group of people he hoped and prayed to join in the future and he stated in collaboration with some of his subordinates laundered the pension funds into his selfish interest.

Likewise, the disgraceful situation of the Accountant General of the Federation who embezzled over ₦110 billion despite his high position, high emoluments, high benefits and sophisticated government facilities he must have been receiving from the contractors who had worked for the government before he released their payments for contacts executed and unexecuted.

Nigerians are the government, they can build a good government and at the same time, they can destroy a good government.

People have been in the government since 2018, about six years ago, government, for reasons best known to their officials, have failed to pay Nigeria Airways' former workers their approved pension balance. You can imagine the suffering the people are going through and their families. We said we all belong to the same country when some people in power of governance could spend ₦148 million to purchase an SUV bulletproof car for their personal use.

In Nigeria, there is nothing like Freedom of Information (FOI) where a journalist or a lawyer can force a minister or member of the Upper Houses to divulge any information on the financial running of the country however crucial and however people might be dying concerning the state of the economy. Probably, the former Accountant General allegedly stole money and has a connection or is part of Nigeria Airways approved pension. The Act that established Nigeria Airways made it a limited liability company, hence the workers of the liquidated airline were not in the same category as applied to the FCAA and NAA workers when it comes to pension regulations. The workers in FCAA and NAA were collecting their pension payments regularly at the end of every month. The worrisome side of the story is that the three organisations were under the same Ministry as parastatals. I am always envious when I meet even the junior workers or an artisan worker of the NAA now FAAN when he tells me how much they earn monthly as a pension. I used to wonder if we were created by the same God for this country or if the workers of the liquidated airline are a special breed that dropped from heaven without a biological parental connection.

The Elephant of Africa in the air once upon a time has been flown to hit the mountain at the highest level and has fallen to the deepest bottom of the sea with so many big bags of granite tied to it so that it will never flow above the sea for the rescuers to see the remnants. The government that established it with pride and pageantry is also the body that destroyed it for selfish interest. As I am writing in 2024, it was eight years since the workers collected the first batch of the ₦78 billion arrears of payment approved by President Buhari, hope of collecting the ₦33 Billion balance still hangs on a very tiny thread as there was never information of hope despite that we lose our members to deaths on illness that should not have taken their lives if the government had done the needful the way it should have been done, at the time it should have been done and to the people it should have been done to. To the majority of the workers of the airline, the light has gone down and the road has been taken over by the flood or tsunami as far as their families are concerned.

The consequence was very devastating as many of our members are continually dying of curable diseases of which, if the pension is made available, the doctors could be consulted for diagnosis and recommended medications for purchases and life could be prolonged. Different families have scattered, separated and divorced as our diagram of history that goes up from year to year begins to descend the marked line. Probably, somebody or the Friday combined prayers of the depressed people in this group at the former catering services would wake up the spirit of President Tinubu on consultation or remind the current Minister of Aviation and Innovation to pity the people who have served their fatherland with integrity and promote the image of the country at national and international level interceded with the indescribable suffering of the pensioners of the former airways.

CHAPTER THIRTY—ONE

MY TRANSVERSE JOURNEYS IN NIGERIA AIRWAYS

I WAS KNOWN for different capacities when I was working for Nigeria Airways and this book does not have my photograph on the front page, I am, therefore, compelled to introduce myself to the readers of this book about how long God had sustained me in the airline and what types of jobs I was assigned during my sixteen years in the service. My name is OLATUNJI OLUSANYA and I was employed and had serviced my period of service in the same department. The department I classified as the class of the poorest in the national airline. As some of the very arrogant, pompous and abusive pilots once said, though very few of them are in this category, they called the people in Personnel as the file carriers. They blame the few gullible ones who have forgotten that all fingers on our hands were never equal and the Lord who created them as they were in different sizes and shapes have specialised functions hence the maker of the human race did not create us in the same complexions, in the same height, with the same intelligent and opportunities to excel were not meant to be equal. Imagine if the races of the people on earth were the same, how could the yellow-coloured people who are called white have the gut to call the chocolate-coloured people "forking black" and the black people call the other yellow-coloured people the "pig"? That is why the wise philosophers said that we should not be thinking alike, reasoning alike and seeing an object alike. The assignments God gave to twin sisters or brothers however identical they might look alike but differed, and they often had different paths to follow from their adulthoods.

When I returned to Nigeria from the United Kingdom in 1979, the Nigeria Electricity Power Authority wanted to offer me employment but as I did not major in accounting subjects, my service was not required by them. But my intention and plan then were If I did not secure employment within my first six months in the country, I would just abandon all the junk people called personal effects and return to the UK. Luckily, I was informed that a vacancy had just been declared open at Nigeria Airways, there and then I submitted my application with my Curriculum Vitae, later interviewed and was found suitable among about ten others who were invited for consideration. The chairman of the panel conducting the interview was the late Tunji Otunuyi of blessed memory, a complete gentleman, well-educated with a Master's degree and very bold and could speak his mind before any director.

As I have said somewhere in the book, I was engaged on grade Level 07 instead of my entitled Grade Level 09 because the budget of the airline was never approved nor returned to the airline months that was supposed to be released to them to implement. There was no year that the airline ever received its approved budget at the time it was supposed to come for its implementation. A desperate hungry man had no choice when offered a meal, the idea that I am a Muslim and hence would not eat pork meat does not come into play when you have no choices to make or that you cannot live close to the Mosque because of their early morning loudspeakers noise in prayers do not come-in if you have built your house before they bought the land to build a Mosque, what choice do you have then to accept it as the design of God for your life.

My first unimaginable and depressive experience came from another Yoruba man whom I should be looking to as an elderly person who was by tradition supposed to play the role of a father's figure. But we are equally born but not equally talented nor equally have respect for our culture and traditions and fail to see other people as human beings and accord them some degree of humanity. Mr Adegoke showed me what some few people of Ibadan were said to be in their gene hatred to the Ijebu people that if you see an Ijebu person and a snake approaching you, you should kill the Ijebu person and let the snake escape away. That could be the philosophy of the Old Testament, as things have changed from Climate Change to the New Testament because the same snake you gave freedom to would come back to kill you and your family. As the late Umaru Dikko wrote about Moshood Kashimawo Abiola during the lives of the two politicians in an article in a magazine, he described the late politician Abiola as a man who had a tiger as his guiding dog and used the same tiger to chase and devoid his political enemies. Subsequently, the tiger has completed its assignment and it remained the two of them in the house, what will the tiger do when he becomes extremely hungry than to turn to his owner and eat him up? That would serve as an end of an era.

Out of disappointment that the panel of interviewers did not employ one of the numerous candidates he gave to them, like King Saul in the Bible, he lost patience and allowed a hot temper and provocations to dominate his spirit, and out of hatred to a man you do not know, you have never seen before and has not offended you in any form he posted me to the Mailing Section. He knew the problems of the section but decided to send me to the tiger cage as he said to Mr Bolade earlier that day so that I would be frustrated and run away or I would make a gross mistake or gross error of judgment and would be sacked. That was a decision I could not reject as I was desperate to start a new life in Nigeria from somewhere after eight years of studying abroad.

At the Mailing section, after a few hours of patiently listening to the people around I noticed and my instincts told me that virtually all the staff in the section were his boys from Mr A, the head of the section to the last person who was the messenger. For the first three weeks, I was merely an attendee studying the procedures as I was second-in-command and I listened and studied the chain of events going in without altering a word of agitation or correction. That is what they call British Diplomacy. Probably that silence created confusion in the workers of the section since they had learnt that I was from abroad. News spread like petrol that ignited a fire. Some of them might be the conduit pipe of information to the controller whom I assumed must have told some of the others to let him know as much as possible about me generally. Mr A was an Ibo guy by State of origin and by name or by parents but was either born in Lagos or has been around the city for a very long time as he speaks the Yoruba language very fluently and with the wonderful proverbs coronations to create sensations some of which I have not heard before. Mr A lived at Fadeyi while I lived in Palm Grove. He was so jovial and without wasting time, we became like twin brothers. Another area of common interest was we all stopped over at the Sky Power Club for one or two bottles of beer almost every day before we proceeded to our areas of abode always in his personal Volkswagen beetle car. In the fourth week, I tried to show the staff that my quietness was no evidence of laziness or cowardice.

There was almost a mountain size of letters addressed to the staff of the airline but their sections or departments of work were not stated, hence they were just dumped in a corner of the office since the individuals are not known to the staff of the section. Without asking questions about why the mails were allowed to be gigantically accumulated as that may result in different stories, I started to pick up the envelopes one by one and started writing "RTS" meaning Return to Sender on them. When the dispatch clerk was going to the post office, I added some of the unknown letters in a moderate batch with the new mail for posting. Within a month, I got rid of virtually all the letters and parcels, but to my surprise, nobody ever made any complaints about my actions. I gave the section a clean and more hygienic environment. Whether they reported me to the controller or not, I never knew and nobody ever asked me questions.

When the Administrative Officer at the Motor Transport abandoned his office because a hoodlum left a juju wrap on his chair, the controller decided to send me to the office probably would eliminate me as everybody knew what the drivers recruited from the garages were made of. All efforts to make him change the posting I approached were fruitless. At the end of the chapter, I had to take it as my destiny and I remembered what Joseph in the Bible went through in the hands of his brothers and the wife of the King of Egypt as he was thrown into the valley to be killed by the lions, later taken up and sold as slave. The wife of the King told fabricated lies against him and was jailed but when the hands of the Lord arose, he became the Prime Minster of Egypt. At the motor transport, the most senior driver was on grade level 05 and that was the driver to the managing director, Captain Tahal. History had it on mouth-to-mouth talks that the captain was the most vulnerable to the driver whenever he was holding the steering. I was also told that his biological brother died in one of his accidents, hence I was very careful in selecting Mr F as his official driver and he was the only driver on grade level 05. There was an office supervisor at the motor transport who was responsible for the monitoring and posting of the drivers in their shift schedules, behaviour and official conduct as reported by the top officials they were driving. The man was a carbon copy in all ramifications of the late Col. Emeka Odumeghu Ojukwu hence he has no other name on the premises than Ojukwu and nobody ever calls him by his biological name of Adelakun. When they were buying cars then Volkswagen Passat cars for the controllers in Engineering and Maintenance, I was able to smuggle the name of Mr Adegoke into the list and he got a car and a full-time driver for his official duties.

Drivers must be drivers, while some are on official duties, we must have some extra drivers at hand in case of emergency assignments. Within six months I was posted to the place, I complied the list of about 12 drivers and pasted their names on the office notice board with a serious warning that their behaviours and performance would no longer be tolerated as at that time their records were nothing to write home about, hence they need to improve on their service or else they would face the disciplinary procedures. Some of the reports I received were that when they sent them on one-hour errands with official vehicles, they could take about six hours or more before they returned to base without any justifiable explanations. Secondly in the car they took out, the extra motor tyres would be replaced with a worn-out one, not to mention the disappearance of jacks, spinners and other tools which were checked to be in the car before they took it out. With the support of the KLM director-in-charge of Engineering and Maintenance, I was able to get rid of reasonable proportions of some of the unruly drivers.

Let me mention just two cases of studies. There was an elderly man in age who was supposed to be a role model to the younger driver but when he got to work, he would be smelling of Indian hemp which he must have taken before coming to work. One Saturday, he was seen by the Controller of Audit at that time Mr Olagunju using an airline VW 27-seaters bus to convey passengers from one of the main junctions along Agege Motor Roads to some villages. The man parked his private car and watched him make about three trips before coming to inform me in the office. I sent one of the supervisors Mr Ashenuga to the area of sighting and he was found to continue in the use of the airline bus for private transportation of passengers. He was asked to report to the office but did not return the bus till Monday morning. When questioned, he said he needed to make some money. Since he was well known in the circle of drivers as somebody who takes Indian Hemp, to avoid violence, I reported the matter to the management and he was sacked.

There was another driver who used to be a personal driver to the late popular Juju musician Ayinde Barrister. On Fridays, he was not dressed in uniform but in a native attire with decorative beads on the neck, on his legs and his wrists. One day, a vehicle was stolen not that of the airline and not on the premises of the airline. The police investigation connected him by information to the incident, when a well in the backyard of his house was searched, they found more than 1000 vehicle plate numbers in the well. He seized to be a staff of the airline.

After I had brought a high standard of discipline to the motor transport section, one Friday, I just received a note from Mr Adegoke on a pad that I was posted away from that office, should report to his office for further instruction and no reason was given. I went to show it to somebody at the managing director's office, and he went to talk with the MD, when he came out, he just told me to go back to continue with my job as they would send him a reply. I was later told that it was the same type of head jotter they used to inform him that my posting was cancelled. That was the end of that story. I have mentioned in one of the chapters where all my staff in the section were retrenched, they picked people from other sections to make up another team of workers for the new section.

MY TRANSVERSE JOURNEYS IN NIGERIA AIRWAYS

My last ten (10) years in the airline were the most challenging, horrific and a trial like that of Joseph in the Bible as I mentioned earlier. By job description, I was in charge of the staff identity cards and that of their families, I was in charge of the staff housings and quarters, in charge of the offices and of the cleaning staff, of the protocol which included welcoming and taking to a hotel, crews of the aircraft chartered to convey our paid passengers from the UK, USA, and Europe to Nigeria. As IATA regulations emphatically stipulated, the crews who managed the plane to Nigeria and those who managed the return journey must have twelve hours of rest in a comfortable hotel. I was to welcome and introduce myself to the crews once they opened their aircraft door I was around to take them to the hotel after they had discharged their passengers. Where there was nobody to assure them of this service, they could shut the door of the plane and return the passengers to where they were coming from. Despite the abuses, insults, and humiliations I used to receive from my co-workers for doing the job with which I have attached the management instruction to the effect, I still receive letters of commendation for a job well down as I did not allow a failure in the performance of the assignments. But unspeakable were two factors:

1. I was supposed to go on duty tours to the places where the airline had stations to sign the staff's identity cards but my last controller would fill out the form for travel in his name and another form for the photographer under my supervision. He would not travel and asked the station managers to sign on my behalf. He would not travel but has collected the overseas

travelling allowance. Thereby I did not collect one American Dollar as extra money while I continued to languish in poverty in Lagos, my controller, my director and the photographer were from the same State of origin,

2. When the time of promotion came, I was convinced beyond reasonable doubt that my director would tell his state-mate my controller that he did not want to see my name cropping up for consideration for promotion. On three occasions promotions were made but I was seen as somebody who did not deserve to earn one. On the third occasion, I went to the director to argue for my right but he told me that my controller was the one who did not include my name in the list of the people he desired to be promoted. I went to challenge my controller, initially, he said my name was on the list then I went back to the director who called Dele, one of his assistants to bring to his office the promotion paper from the General Affairs, my name was conspicuously not on the list. Then common sense and diplomacy told me something was wrong somewhere. I did not bulge myself again from that point. That was part of my destiny I assumed.

Historically, I was an active member in the trade union activities of the airline but was ever cautious of my position with the management team of the department I was working. Hence, I always avoided holding an elected position but played my role as an active father figure without a face. When we were in NUATSE, I was rewarded with a 5-week union training course in Czechoslovakia before the country was politically split into two countries Czech and Slovakia as known today. My co-active members then include Mr Onabanjo and Mr Odeyemi who are now residing in the United States of America. To form the ATSSSAN, I was also an active member who recommended that we should seek the interference of Lawyer Femi Falana to face the management of the airline to recognise the senior staff union.

During my service, several times that opportunity opened for personnel staff to seek departmental transfer to other departments where people see as juicy and more lucrative to do and the future looked promising and many men and women seized the opportunity of cross over but my instinct and knowledge of the airline then showed me that when retrenchment exercise arrived in December, such newcomers or new faces often become the first whose names would be listed as they were often seen as spies or intruders. In earnest, they were all wiped out of their new places from security, ground operations and marketing.

The little and few promotions I had had to do with my self-disciple, self-respect and determination not to worship no man or go to the bosses' houses to tell fake and unfounded stories about others in consideration for promotions. Though I was overlooked on so many opportunities to progress within the ladder of management God vindicated me and instead of being sacked or running away within three months of employment as predicted, I was able to live and narrate what I experienced about life in the airline in a book is a praise to the Lord. That is a big achievement than all the golds and silvers in the world and a big pride to the Lord my maker.

There was one typical scenario at the cash office that could not erase its impact on my life, as I was entering the office of the cash office one day, a lady from the audit office was exiting. Probably the audit lady must have heard the workers discussing the approved memo I had deposited at the cash office which has gone through the scrutiny of their section, and the amount of American Dollars on it to host the crews of the chartered flight the airline was expecting the following morning at 05:00, she must have dropped some irresponsible statement of bombshell. As I entered the office, one of the clerks probably of the same age as my son, told me in a loud and unmixing clear statement to the hearing of everybody in the office both the workers and other visitors, and I quoted him, "You always come here to worry us about money, and we have been informed that when you leave the airline, you will not get "KOBO" as gratuity and pension" I was shocked, irritated and ashamed, but when I considered that I have a national assignment at hand, I pretended as if he was not addressing me. If the flight could be flying back to the country it originated, through my failure, the airline would be castigated by the public, the airline would dismiss me from the service and the country would have another bad image and reputation to the outside world.

Just as he completed his castigation on me, the manager of the office Alhaji Fana stepped out of his office, when he saw me in some distance, he told me he had authorised the staff to release the money to me, to the hearing of everybody. That silences everybody and I need not make any report of anybody, what do I gain in getting anybody into administrative trouble? That was just one of so many situations I had to endure at the hands of other employees of the same organisation. I left the company voluntarily with a clean record after sixteen years and am proud to say I am on the list of pensioners the government has failed to pay the balance of their pension payments.

On three occasions, God saved me from the network of armed robbers or house burglaries which were popular then. To get to the airport before 05:00 in the morning, I have to leave my residence around 03:30 in the morning and on these occasions, I narrowly escape falling into the hands of these marauders. That danger does not concern the other staff who are just required to do their pen-pushing assignments nor the airline management whose concern was to query me if I failed to carry out the assignment as contributory impediments of the other workers are not acceptable as an excuse to them as an explanation for the failure.

ABOUT THE AUTHOR

As indicated in the book, no changes have been made to my original account. I served the airline from 1979 to 1995, leaving when the work environment, particularly within Human Resources, became unbearable. While working as an Administrative Officer in the Motor Transport section, I often stayed late to ensure all vehicles on assignment returned to base. Unfortunately, some drivers exploited the system by swapping new tyres with worn ones and stealing essential tools like spanners and jacks daily.

After I transferred out of Motor Transport, the section was taken over by Mr. Ewurum, who replaced me with his kinsman, Ugbaja. This experience taught me that life is often a cycle that demands endurance. At the General Affairs section, I dedicated myself to excellence and made it a point to avoid any situations that could lead to blame or disciplinary actions. Leading a sharp team required extra effort and vigilance. On Sundays, after church, I would drop by the office to review the contents of my staff's desks. I occasionally found unauthorised documents, especially relating to family registrations, and discreetly noted them for follow-up. My diligence ensured that any potential issues were addressed without confrontation, as it is

ABOUT THE AUTHOR

often the person who signs off on improper paperwork who faces the consequences, not the one who prepares it.

I also served as a Protocol Officer, managing logistics for foreign aircraft hired to transport passengers. On several occasions, I had to process requests for funds in U.S. dollars to accommodate international flight crews at the Sheraton Hotel, as the hotel would not accept payments in Naira or offer credit. Navigating the airline's bureaucracy was often frustrating, with sections treating my requests as though I were seeking personal benefits. Despite these challenges, I persevered, regularly meeting flight crews at the airport as early as 5:00 a.m. and staying on-site until their aircraft cleared Nigerian airspace. On three occasions, I narrowly escaped armed robbery attempts while commuting in the early hours.

Despite my dedication, I was overlooked for promotion for eight years, even though others at my level were promoted every three years, as long as they had no performance issues. After being excluded from the promotion list for the third time, I sought answers from the Director of Human Resources, only to discover that my name had mysteriously been left off the list. Although Mr. Alabi, a fellow officer, assured me my name was submitted, it was clear there was a conspiracy to block my advancement. Despite commendations from my controller for my flawless work, my efforts were never recognised. It became evident that my exclusion might have been influenced by regional biases.

A turning point came when a non-staff individual tried to travel abroad using a fraudulent airline staff ticket and identity card. An investigation into the incident was initiated, and I was unfairly implicated. The Director of Human Resources even recommended my dismissal without allowing me to defend myself. Fortunately, a departmental messenger confessed during the disciplinary hearing, revealing the real perpetrators of the ticket fraud and clearing my name. Although the Director expressed his frustration at not being able to penalise me, I left the hearing with my integrity intact.

Throughout my career, I was actively involved in union activities. I attended trade union training in Czechoslovakia before it split into two nations and helped establish the senior staff union (ATSSSAN). However, due to the hostility I faced from Human Resources, I declined any executive roles that might put me at risk of retrenchment. I also served as General Secretary of both the Sky Power Social Club and the Nigeria Airways Cooperative Society, often playing a key role in decision-making and governance. Though I was never elected President or Chairman, possibly due to financial constraints, I was repeatedly entrusted with the role of General Secretary because of my dedication and reliability.

MAY GOD HELP ME
WITH MY PEN.